12 LAWS
of the
JUNGLE

12 LAWS
of the
JUNGLE

HOW to BECOME a LETHAL ENTREPRENEUR

DANIEL CLELAND

HOUNDSTOOTH
PRESS

12 LAWS OF THE JUNGLE
How to Become a Lethal Entrepreneur

ISBN   978-1-5445-2732-1   *Hardcover*

      978-1-5445-2730-7   *Paperback*

      978-1-5445-2731-4   *Ebook*

      978-1-5445-2733-8   *Audiobook*

Contents

I intend for this book to teach the entrepreneurial knowledge and experience I've gained in my ten years of battle in the world of SME entrepreneurship. I dedicate this work to every young man and woman who wishes to free themselves from the confines of low cash and low freedom to achieve a lifestyle of high impact and high optionality. The surest way to de-victimize yourself is to build your successful business and achieve the freedom that your heart desires.

Foreword

Patrick Bet-David

READING DANIEL CLELAND'S BOOK IS A WORTHWHILE investment. I don't say that often so let me unpack it for you.

As the creator of Valuetainment and a founder/CEO myself, I come in contact with tens of thousands of entrepreneurs. Of those I meet, a small percentage are great leaders. An even smaller percentage are great creators with real imagination and the ability to see things others can't.

Daniel is the rare entrepreneur who is both a creative and a doer. What struck me most when I met Daniel is that we share a passion for changing mindsets. As you're about to see in *12 Laws of the Jungle,* neither of us can stand victimhood, and we see entrepreneurship as the fastest path to achieving freedom.

As you might expect, this book has a lot in common with Daniel. First off, it's full of adventure. He tells a story of how, on a drunken impulse, he climbed a sixty-five-foot cliff in Australia. Though I'm not going to give away the conclusion, I can tell you that it did not end well.

The book is also packed with real business tools that every entrepreneur needs. And more than anything, the book has heart. You can almost feel Daniel pouring his heart out on the page, encouraging you to give your best and follow the same path that he used to achieve financial freedom while building a heart-centered business.

Go through Daniel's Instagram and you'll see this ripped, tattooed guy living an amazing life. In one pic, he's got a monkey on his shoulder; in the next a guitar; and in the next, he's in an ice bath! You look at this guy and think he's living the dream. Like most people you see on Instagram, you wonder if he actually is. It's only because I've seen Daniel during both his highs and lows (processing business issues with him) that I can tell you that he's the real deal. Plus, I think what makes living the dream that much sweeter for Daniel is that he had to suffer a lot to get there. He's a self-made guy who isn't afraid to share how tough things got for him.

Unlike most authors, Daniel doesn't just share the good. Right when his business peaked, COVID hit. In his words, it was like "waking up in a business nightmare." That experience, as much as any, will show you how to deal with the adversity that every entrepreneur will face.

Daniel is honest, vulnerable, and real. In Chapter One, he tells you what entrepreneurship is actually like. "It's ugly; it's very lonely; it's very frustrating; and it exploits you at the highest level." When I read this, I thought I couldn't have said it any better myself. Then I realized that he was quoting me! That's the truth, and both Daniel and I aren't afraid to share it with you. As a result, you'll learn, from someone who is in the arena, what to do when your world turns upside down.

12 Laws of the Jungle will keep you turning the page because you'll feel like you're riding shotgun on his amazing journey. One minute, he's backstage at a rock concert; the next, he's running his retreat center in Costa Rica; and before you know it, he's on the red carpet for a movie premiere in New York City.

An important thing for you to know is that I have never tried ayahuasca. Whether you have or haven't, this book is incredibly valuable. Ultimately, it's the business lessons that will keep you highlighting the pages and giving you the tools to create your own success.

Because Daniel was so clear on his vision, he became the rare entrepreneur to build a business that checked all the boxes: profit, passion, fun, and meaning. If you're after the same, you need to read this book.

The future looks bright! And it's even brighter if you read this book carefully.

Patrick Bet-David
Entrepreneur and creator of Valuetainment
#1 Wall Street Journal bestselling
author of *Your Next Five Moves*

Introduction

THE LETHAL ENTREPRENEUR

February 19, 2020

Denver, Colorado

The Twenty-Five-Year Reunion Tour
for Machine Head

I HAD NEVER HEARD OF THE WORD *ENTREPRENEURSHIP*.

At sixteen years of age, I wouldn't have had a clue what it meant. Maybe it was a French dessert. The only thing I was sure of was I was going to be a rock star, following the footsteps of one of my all-time favorite guitarists, the legendary Logan Mader (formerly of Machine Head and Soulfly, and now Once Human). I couldn't have guessed "entrepreneurship" was going to make him my friend.

Now, at age thirty-eight, I was backstage with Logan, sharing the rum I brought from Costa Rica. He had put aside an all-access

1

backstage pass so I could soak in the twenty-five-year reunion tour of their 1995 hit album (one of my favorites) for free. To my astonishment, we became friends a few months earlier when he expressed his desire to do an ayahuasca retreat at my company, *Soltara Healing Center*.

I'd flown down to the concert in Denver as an *entrepreneur* of all things, halfway into a ten-day business trip that was going to carry my company further into a league of its own. Just days earlier, I was in New York City where I'd been invited to the premiere of *ReConnect: The Movie*—a documentary made by the notorious entrepreneur Brian Rose about his spiritual adventure trying the plant medicine, ayahuasca. Thanks to years of intense effort perfecting our ayahuasca retreats, my company, Soltara, had become THE retreat center of choice for the movie—it's where Brian drank the sacred medicine. As Soltara's CEO, I was proud seeing my two-year-old company up there on screen, changing Brian's life. But I was even more stoked to know it was going to do the same for a legendary guitarist and four-time, gold-album producer I'd been looking up to since I was sixteen.

On the night of the concert, I hung out with Logan and the whole band. I even met the singer, Robb Flynn! Euphoric is the only word that comes close. Before leaving, Logan and I shook hands on the agreement that he and his wife, Lauren Hart (lead singer of Once Human), would join us just weeks later in Costa Rica for a retreat, after which we'd all take a trip to the beach and hang there a few days. A dream come true.

That mind-blowing experience is what sparked my idea to write this book. I'd just watched my life come full circle thanks to the powers of entrepreneurship. Unbeknownst to my sixteen-year-old self, life had wildly different ideas for me than becoming a rock star. It dragged me through fifteen confusing years and a handful of ayahuasca ceremonies until I realized I was meant to slam a dent into the universe by becoming an entrepreneur. Plus, another eight years hacking my way through the entrepreneurial jungle to learn how to do so with lethal effectiveness. I now felt highly confident I could voice my methodology in a book made for the next wave of entrepreneurs and go-getters: aka YOU!

That book idea grew from a spark to an explosion during the final days of my business trip. After Logan's concert, I flew to Las Vegas for the 10X conference (hosted by Grant Cardone). It was *really* next level. Sitting in the VIP section, I watched ultra-successful millionaires and billionaires like Floyd Mayweather, John Travolta, Dana White, Magic Johnson, and others walk on the stage. They all shared their advice on how to 10X life and break through to the next level of the game. It moved me, to say the least. If before the conference I had felt confident, after the conference I felt confident *and* insanely motivated. My time had come. I was ready to return home to Costa Rica and begin the writing process.

This book in your hands was meant to lay out the exact methodology I used during the years 2017–2020 to build the business of my dreams (Soltara Healing Center), position it as a Top 3 Ayahuasca Center in the world, actualize my dream life, and teach others how you can apply the methodology toward your conquests too. But, similar to my rock star ambitions, that book didn't happen either.

As I walked into LAX airport to catch my return flight and start on the book, I could feel paranoia in the air. There were no confirmed cases in the USA, but people had heard the news about "that thing from China" called COVID-19, starting to spread carnage in other countries, and I could sense the latent unease among travelers now. Sideways glances. A little extra sanitizer at the bar. A little extra space in between luggage bags. A little extra cringe at the general filthiness of the LAX airport. There was a real possibility it was here.

I was in denial. Soltara JUST finished our best month of revenues and profits in history (February 2020). I was JUST beginning to live the dream I set out to accomplish at the beginning of my entrepreneurial journey. After my plane landed and I arrived home, I was hellbent on keeping our streak going at least through April and getting through Logan's retreat. There were no cases in Costa Rica, after all.

Until there were.

Everybody on this planet has their own COVID-19 story, and I'm sure you're no different. But for me, it came at the most frustrating of times. Just as everything was starting to roll with Soltara and I was getting ready to tell my story of "how I made it and how you can too," COVID-19 sprung up like a spring daisy during the first two weeks of March. It quickly went from "that thing in China" to "that thing in China, Iran, and Italy" to "that thing fucking everywhere!"

The world turned upside down. My world turned upside down. If during my business trip I was looking at clear skies and smooth sailing to the promised land, then on March 16 I was looking at a total moratorium on travel, society gripped by confusion and fear, and the obliteration of all Soltara retreats.

THIS BOOK

The weeks that followed were like waking up in a business nightmare. The inspiring experiences I had enjoyed at Logan's concert, the *ReConnect* premier, and the 10X conference (all dreams come true in their own way) were disintegrating into the past. During my business trip, I rode around in ominous black Escalades, stayed at the Whitby Hotel executive suite in NYC, and soaked in the benefits of having built Soltara into a globally respected healing center–I finally became the "plant medicine entrepreneur who made it!" But alas, once COVID wrapped itself around the world and my business with impossible tightness (this book cover embodies that fight to the death), I was fast becoming "the plant medicine entrepreneur who won't make it if these borders don't reopen ASAP."

Like the rest of the world, COVID complicated my identity and life path. As CEO, I had to assume the new role of prepper, which meant switching gears urgently. I had to make sure that Soltara had an emergency survival plan that would give my team a place to live on-premises, and I'd have to buy a stock of food to weather an indefinite storm with ZERO revenue. To make matters worse, how was I supposed to write a book on "how I made it"? At the rate things were going, it was possible the book would end up reading like an obituary for my company.

The problem: I'd already partnered with Matt Cartagena to help write the book. As the founder of UnpackGenius, Matt specializes in "unpacking the genius" from busy entrepreneurs and leaders like myself who don't have time to undergo the hard trekking required to make a legendary product. He's lethal at creating books and courses audiences love. By this point, we'd already unpacked the book blueprint and a feast of business stories that happened from 2017–2020 in the building of Soltara. It was gonna be hard to cancel on him.

"What blessings can come from the lockdown?" Matt questioned me during one of our next interviews.

I try to find the silver lining in everything, and most times I do. I believe there is a yin for every yang, and that's what the best entrepreneurs know. But this time, I couldn't see it. I told him how I really felt about that question, "COVID is a fucking nightmare disaster and nothing good can possibly come from this!"

After a couple days passed, and I grudgingly began solving our way out of the abyss of death, Matt's question finally took root in my mind. Whenever I would turn my attention to solving a new business problem brought on by COVID, I noticed that the entrepreneurial methods I originally planned to teach in this book were proving to be my strongest allies. Day by day, COVID was pressuring me to use them again, but more aggressively this time with nothing held back and taken to their absolute limit. It all clicked. COVID wasn't just a nightmare; it was the life-and-death arena to put my methodology to the ultimate test, sharpen it, and turn it into a more lethal weapon for all trailblazers like you.

And test it, I did.

Matt and I developed a process to record *everything* I was learning from my business battles vs. the COVID lockdowns. During the day, I made moves on the "business chessboard" and watched as the ever-shifting pandemic punched back with counterattacks. Then, come nighttime, Matt and I identified every pattern, story, and "Law" of entrepreneurship I observed that day. It turned out to be the wartime journaling I never did in my past years—in the trenches, play-by-play, entrepreneurship through my eyes.

When we first began this book, I remember telling Matt something one of my Peruvian friends, a prolific jungle guide named Victor, used to say to me, "In the jungle, your machete is your best friend. If you wander out into the jungle without your machete, you won't last forty-eight hours before something or other kills you." In the end, this book became more than I could've imagined—a machete for all entrepreneurs, intrapreneurs, solopreneurs, and rebels looking to enter the jungle of business (or life) and win their holy grail. Hence why I titled the book *12 Laws of the Jungle*.

The chapters (the Laws) inside teach not only how we built Soltara to pre-COVID success, but ALSO how we navigated the worst crisis in our lifetime to actually come out stronger and better on the other side. After all, it's not enough to want to 10X our life. We must have staying power and advance our journey under any circumstance. Throughout my ten years of entrepreneurship, I've done that to the best of my ability. Until this book, my methods only existed in my head. Now, thanks to the pandemic, they are in your hands and sharper than ever.

I promise that if you use these 12 Laws like a glorious machete, they will help you achieve your dream life, and you'll emerge stronger from all challenges. One major lesson I (re)learned from the pandemic is our dreams don't manifest by accident. In fact, our dreams reserve themselves for those who are daring enough to troop into the jungle, endure the ruthless elements, and keep taking enormous action. You can bet there are lethal forces in there waiting for you who are hungry to infect your mind with doubt and bring you to your knees. You can also bet this book was written to defeat them.

HOW TO READ THE LAWS

These Laws are not for people who blame success on "privilege" or who adopt a victim mentality. That mindset is sure to sabotage what I'm teaching here, so I won't waste your time. In fact, if you suffer from those diseases of the mind, don't waste your time here either.

These Laws are written exclusively for the LETHAL ENTRE-PRENEUR: anybody who has the guts to confront fear, conquer it by any means, and achieve their Fuck Yes! Life.

These Laws are written for those willing to make SACRIFICES in the name of building their legendary company, income stream, or life adventure.

These Laws are written for those who are DONE wasting precious hours.

These Laws are for those ready to go ALL IN on becoming their ultimate self.

While this book focuses mainly on business events, you should know that the word "entrepreneur" comes from the French word *entreprendre* (*not* a French dessert), which means to undertake. In that sense, "entrepreneur" is simply a code name for anybody choosing to succeed in their undertaking. So, more widely, this book is for those who wish to bring any creative project to life, improve their personal practice, or win bigger in their self-employment—anybody smack in the middle of their Hero's Journey.

How should you apply the Laws in your life? Personally, I find that most situations on the hard road to success fall into the realm of one or another, or combinations of these Laws, and on any given day the applicable Law(s) can be used to beat your adversary, win your objective, or get you out of a bind:

- *Law 1 (The Jungle Doesn't Care)* upgrades your mental strength so you won't be beaten by the ruthless forces of business and life.

- *Law 2 (Shape Your Mind to Warfare)* teaches you how to navigate the jungle like a military general, remaining calm and calculated when making do-or-die decisions.

- *Law 3 (Learn to Hunt)* unlocks your greatest power as an entrepreneur—the art of selling and influencing—and teaches how to use it for the good of your village (aka your operation).

- *Law 4 (Set Your Destination)* stokes the fire in your belly, in your decisions, in your strategies, and in your thoughts with an authentic Vision for your Fuck Yes! Life.

- *Law 5 (Map Your Route)* gets you thinking like a chess grandmaster by showing you how to concoct a strategy that keeps you making substantial progress in your Fuck Yes! Life (every fiscal quarter).

- *Law 6 (Build Your Masterful Tribe)* walks you through the stages of building a team and inner circle that's strong enough to push your company (and Vision) uphill over the mountain of greatness.

- *Law 7 (Plan for Snakebites)* brings you face to face with every entrepreneur's peskiest foe—the snakebite (aka setbacks)—and shows how to mitigate their harm.

- *Law 8 (Master Your Resources)* gets to the bare essence of survival: how to master your financial resources so your team always has fuel to endure and prosper in the startup war.

- *Law 9 (Sharpen Your Spear)* teaches how to always be ready for the one-shot, one-kill business opportunity that will walk into your crosshairs (and won't stay long).

- *Law 10 (The Time to Kill Is Now)* sets you apart from 99 percent of people by teaching how to unleash your Kill Instinct.

- *Law 11 (Let the Village Eat First)* proves that you are NOTHING without your tribe and shows how to keep them driven throughout the entire startup war.

- *Law 12 (Prepare for Winter)* hammers home the inescapable reality that disasters happen, and you must already have a Winter Fortress built for when the next one happens.

While these Laws are centered around COVID, the examples and instructions are timeless. This year it's COVID; next year it could be anything. COVID was simply an amplified petri dish for watching these Laws propagate. They are useful in any business, any creative challenge, and any environment. When the next "big one" lands, it's going to pay to have this machete by your side.

Prior to the pandemic, these Laws endowed Soltara (and my previous business, Pulse) with the holy grail of a tourism business over the years: full bookings, great margins, super-strong brand, smooth operations, sustainable seven figures, en route to eight figures. But it didn't stop there. It also endowed me with an adventurous entrepreneurial spirit—a fact that dawned on me after a podcast host heard my startup tales and called me "The Indiana Jones of Entrepreneurship."

While I cannot deny liking that name just a little bit, I'm way more interested in passing the glorious machete (and whip) to you. YOU are the next legend of startups. YOU are the Indiana Jones of Entrepreneurship. YOU have a startup adventure with your name written on it. I believe that great entrepreneurs are the soldiers of capitalism responsible for ushering in a new era of sustainability and peace on our planet. So, I want YOU to get after it! I'm here to help.

But, beware. There are no guarantees in this jungle. You will be challenged again and again. So be ready to go all the way. Not 95 percent. Not 99 percent. Not 99.9999 percent. All. Fucking. In.

Read it again. I mean it. ALL. FUCKING. IN.

Because once you start, you can't back out. I don't care how much it starts to hurt. If you back out, you fail in the ugliest possible way. There will be no backing out. Not on my watch.

Ready? Pause before answering. Because if that question makes you overly nervous, then maybe you aren't ready for entrepreneurship. Sure, it is great to take on challenges, but it is stupid to go on a suicide mission. If instead the question exhilarates you, congratulations, your adventure is off to a promising start.

More than ever, I believe the world needs strong leaders like you, yet they exist in such short supply. My guess is because leaders are not born; leaders make themselves! If you're ready for that adventure, it means you will need to reinvent yourself, again and again, under what seem like impossible conditions. So hold this weapon tight. You are about to enter the jungle and become all you were meant to become.

It is with great pleasure I introduce you to Law One.

Law 1

THE JUNGLE DOESN'T CARE

> *"This is a ruthless world and one must be ruthless to cope with it."*
>
> —Charlie Chaplin

There is no time to waste. I will break the news to you straight. Before you have any chance of carrying your company to prosperity, there is a dirty secret about entrepreneurship:

> The game of entrepreneurship is so ugly that if people actually knew how ugly it was upfront, very few would even do it. It's ugly, it's very lonely, it's very frustrating, and it exploits you at the highest level. In the world of business, you don't just have one or two weaknesses, imagine 50 weaknesses are exposed all at the same time, and everybody tells you, because it's YOU. And imagine a game where you ALWAYS have to recreate yourself, or else you lose.[1]

---

1 Patrick Bet-David, interview with Brian Rose on London Real, April 19, 2019, https://www.youtube.com/watch?v=gokQGbl-OX4.

That was an all-important quote from Patrick Bet-David (PBD), the founder of Valuetainment (+2.5Mill YouTube subscribers). He is one of the most relentless entrepreneurs in the game. He is a man I respect enormously. A man who built his empire from nothing. He began as an immigrant from Iran, then went to the Army, then followed that with eleven years of relentless entrepreneurship until (as of the writing of this book), he grew his financial services company to over $100Mill.

That is to say, he *knows* entrepreneurship. And from my experience building companies, his quote is 100 percent accurate. But do you know what is not accurate? Media and Instagram portrayals. They perpetuate the belief that entrepreneurs fly in helicopters, drive yachts like playboys or playgirls, sitting there effortlessly, drinking champagne as their passive income makes them rich. I'm here to call bullshit on that narrative. And as you progress on your journey, I recommend you ignore that narrative too and swallow the red pill of entrepreneurship instead:

Law 1: The jungle doesn't care if you live or die.

Nor does the market.

That's the ever-present rule of this game. Entrepreneurship is not your friend; it's like the Amazon jungle. And if you wander into entrepreneurship without your machete and right expectations, you won't last forty-eight hours before one thing or another kills you. You vanish into business extinction. Gone. Taken out by whatever is hungry that day.

The jungle of entrepreneurship is ruthless: it doesn't care about your exciting idea, financial crisis, 10,000+ likes on Instagram, marital problems, or even the next version of COVID-19. It's the *marketplace* with its gauntlet of challenges that you will face: life-changing decisions; a never-ending stack of bills; competitors strategizing to steal your market share; bad actors trying to exploit your company's pockets; employees looking to you for answers, and for their paycheck. These forces don't stop coming. They've been eating companies before you arrived. They will keep eating companies after you exit.

The jungle of entrepreneurship is uncomfortable: while this game may become comfortable (and prosperous if you play your cards right for a few years), real entrepreneurs know that portrayals often overlook the sleepless nights, stress-induced health scares, early mornings, tough choices, covert failures (aka ones you cover up), tears, addictions, and more. Not everybody is cut out for this warrior lifestyle.

Maybe all this sounds daunting, but now that we've exposed the truth, you should also know *that's* what makes entrepreneurship an adventure. Think a level deeper about Patrick Bet-David's quote: if the game of entrepreneurship is so "ugly," then why have millions of self-made entrepreneurs marched the path? Why has PBD stayed in such a ruthless game? Why should you?

I believe the answer is in every entrepreneur's heart: the desire to build their own empire. Every entrepreneur has experienced the moment when it *"hit them."* Maybe they were a kid, in their twenties, or older in life, but it *hit* them—that uncontrollable desire to free themselves from the bondage of low cash, low freedom, low options, and low impact on the world. Whatever the impetus, it pushed them to take life into their own hands and build freedom, wealth, and joy into their life. I remember my "moment" began seeping in years ago when I was selling solar panels in Canada (where I'm from). It dawned on me then that there were only two ways I was going to achieve the financial freedom I longed for: either get really good at a sales job with uncapped commissions or build a business that generates abundance in my life.

If you've read this far, chances are that the "moment" hit you already. In Law 4 you'll turn that urge for a bigger, better, more fulfilling life into a detailed Vision for your Fuck Yes! Life. But before getting ahead of yourself, let's address the holy mammoth in the room: how will you *guarantee* you never get eaten by the jungle before all that happens? Like I mentioned in the introduction, there will be no suicide missions on my watch!

I believe the key is in forging your unbreakable spirit *before* entering the jungle. Like a tree, if you never endured stressful winds in your lifetime, you would snap at the first gust of a bad storm. Instead, you should habituate yourself to the jungle's ruthlessness by throwing yourself into storms, recovering, and then growing stronger. This way, when the hurricane hits, you are the last one standing. That's the goal.

The way to forge an unbreakable spirit is by completing what I call *The Passage*. Think of it like earning your license to navigate entrepreneurship. The Passage is any challenge(s) which pushes you to your absolute breaking point and holds you there until you have some kind of spiritual awakening or visceral epiphany of who you are. It proves to you–beyond doubt–that you're strong enough to go through deep waters (rough, dark, stressful places) and survive them. After completing your Passage, you possess a heightened sense of self-assurance, knowing that you can handle whatever life throws at you.

There were more than a few moments while growing Soltara when the words *I wish I didn't start this fucking thing* sat on the tip of my tongue: the moment I was being extorted by local government (imagine hearing the words "$50K, or we throw you in jail"); the moment my team was burning out, bleeding cash, and weeks away from financial insolvency; the moment when our breaking points had us by the throat. Thankfully, I had already completed my Passage in the years leading up to those moments, so I never allowed my tongue to utter the words sitting on it. However, I know for a fact if I *didn't* turn my skin to leather by walking the Passage, Soltara would have survived neither those tough times nor COVID-19.

These next four sections depict how I *did* complete it.

In 2006 I realized I needed to. I couldn't lie to myself. I was a twenty-five-year-old white man, raised in rural Canada, and I had never tasted real adversity in my life. Sure, I collected bumps and scratches in my history, but nothing that answered the question lurking in my mind: can I go ALL THE WAY if I need to? That question and my growing lust for adventure made me leave Canada to start exploring the world. Little did I know it would initiate me into a five-year journey around the world that would undergird my future as an entrepreneur. Your Passage needn't take so long, but it should have the same effect.

Treat the following sections as your portable *Four Habits of Highly Lethal Entrepreneurs*. The tales you're about to read are by no means everything I went through after leaving Canada (for that, you can read my first book, *Pulse of the Jungle*). Here, I have omitted various heartbreaks, psychedelic experiences, stints as a tour guide, boat working, business experiments, and other challenges. However, I made sure to include the crucial challenges and lessons in my life that can help shape you into an able-bodied entrepreneur. The jungle doesn't care if you live or die, but it certainly respects those who won't break.

BECOME YOUR #1 CRITIC

The challenge that really accelerated my Passage happened in Brisbane, Australia on the night of November 27, 2009. I flew there six months earlier on an errant whim to pursue higher education, love, and adventure. Well, none of that worked out, and by November I was an emotional disaster, drowning my sorrows on the regular. That night, on drunken impulse, I decided to climb a sixty-five-foot cliff with no strategy of any kind. One o'clock in the morning. Alone. Wasted. Wearing dress shoes. What was my thinking? Just prove to myself I could reach the top.

After climbing fifty-five feet, I realized my foolishness. I reached an impasse and panicked. My grip was failing. My knees were shaking. I could see the top. I just couldn't get there. I tried scaling back down but my dress shoes kept slipping on the rocks. I looked down and instantly knew this fall could kill me. Having nowhere to go but up, I lurched for the next rock, missed it, and fell like a rock all the way down.

The impact rerouted my life forever. My femur busted out, barely missed my femoral artery, destroyed my pelvis, and left me with severe nerve damage from the waist down. And yes, that meant I could no longer feel my baby-maker. Lying in the hospital bed, I asked doctors if the nerve damage would repair itself. They told me, "Nerve damage can take up to eighteen months to heal, if ever." I was living in hell now. Excruciating pain. Undying regret. No end in sight. Stranded in that hospital bed, I had absolutely no choice but to face what I'd been running from all those years: *myself.*

That's your first challenge. No, not taking foolish risks and hurting yourself. I'm talking about *facing yourself* and—in time—building a brutal level of self-awareness. Think again to what Patrick Bet-David said earlier in this chapter, "In the world of business you don't just have one or two weaknesses, imagine 50 weaknesses are exposed all at the same time, and everybody tells you, because it's you!" In other words, if *you* don't expose your weaknesses and mitigate them, the jungle of business (and life) will do it for you. That's what really happened to me in Australia: life caught up to me.

Facing yourself is about becoming your #1 Critic: appraising your inner game *constantly*, smoking out your weaknesses, staring in the mirror, and identifying where you need to grow. Don't get me wrong; it isn't about becoming pessimistic or drowning in the negatives. On the contrary. It's about *optimistic realism*—a life-long habit which empowers you to evolve in the jungle, life, and relationships. Without it, the jungle (and its endless cycle of problems) registers you as the doe-eyed Bambi and slams pressure upon your blind spots. Trust me, you don't want that, especially when your company is on your shoulders.

Of course, there are mechanisms to *force* you into facing yourself, and better ones than tumbling down a cliff. If you have never faced a super challenging experience (one that takes you into deep waters), I advise you to choose your own mechanism: do a ten-day vipassana meditation retreat, or do a physical undertaking like martial arts, or buy a Morozko Forge ice bath and try sitting for twenty minutes per day. There are tons of things to expose your inner game. The important part is to pick one that feels natural, learn from it, and take your inner game into your own hands.

My "mechanism" happened to be an involuntary forty-day/night battle versus the hospital bed. It was long, unforgiving, even emasculating. But eventually my nerves did repair and my baby-maker did begin functioning normally again. The *full* road to recovery (which spanned many months) exposed all sorts of inner demons and weaknesses I had previously swept under the rug. Namely, my secret opinions about myself, my patterns of self-sabotage, the downward slope I'd been on for years but masked by my addictions. More than anything, it forced me to stop lying to myself and realize I couldn't keep living the way I had been living. I had to recreate myself.

GRADUATE FROM PRESSURE

Pressure is the air you breathe in the jungle. Think again about PBD's quote *"...imagine a game where you always have to recreate yourself,* **or else** *you lose."* He is speaking here about pressure and the constant element in business. The entrepreneurs who win big aren't necessarily the ones with the highest IQ. The graveyard of business is filled with very talented ex-founders.

The victors, on the other hand, often are the ones who learn to inhale the pressure and turn it into growth.

Which brings me to your second challenge: graduate from pressure. In the "worker lifestyle," you may get a pass for staying in the lower grades of your psychological, physical, and spiritual maturity. But in the game of entrepreneurship, you must graduate from yesteryear's pressure. Every quarter you get slammed with higher stakes, more advanced problems, and less sympathetic forces. But if embraced, the same pressures have the power to turn your company, team, and you into diamonds.

Here's a "microdose" approach for getting comfortable with the uncomfortable:

Step 1: Identify an area where you're stagnating, avoiding, or needing growth. The previous section should've highlighted this for you.

Step 2: Add an "or else!" Bet money on yourself (stickk.com is a great resource to put your money where your mouth is), or announce your goal to social media (especially friends who will judge you harshly if you fail), or put yourself in harm's way a little more (if you're doing a physical undertaking, pick a scarier opponent or challenge). Ultimately, your job is to attach painful consequences to your failure.

Step 3: Win or fail. There's one question to judge if you handled the pressure: *"Did you succeed under the new pressure?"* Business building often comes down to that question. Failed under pressure? Then you have work to do and stress tolerance to build. Rinse and repeat until you overcome this microdose of pressure.

After you do, you'll feel relieved, knowing that you upgraded your pressure-bearing skills.

If you're up for the challenge, ancient medicine like ayahuasca is great training. One, it is uniquely challenging. Two, you learn how to handle stress from another dimension. Three, you learn what you truly want out of life. Nobody can tell you if you're ready for ayahuasca; only you can hear if it's calling. For example, after my cliff accident in Australia, I heard it loud and clear.

Desperate to forever banish the sabotage, fear, and regret which had been dominating my life thus far, I decided to upgrade myself by whatever means necessary. Luckily, I had read about ayahuasca a few years before my hospital stay and began following a counterculture website. The website kept describing it as a plant medicine with tremendous healing powers. Before my accident, that's all ayahuasca was to me: an interesting idea for self-healing. But after my accident, ayahuasca was screaming my name. After all, I'd almost just died and was completely unsure about what was next for me. What did I have to lose?

In August of 2010, a few months after I could walk again, I found myself in New Mexico for my first ayahuasca ceremony. My goal was to test myself like never before. I got what I asked for because it turned out to be the most intense challenge I had ever experienced, by far. After drinking the medicine, it transported me to the psychedelic gauntlet: that physically safe space you can visit and put yourself through the wringer. That liminal place where you *want* to quit; you *want* the pressure to stop; but it *won't* stop until you achieve dominion over your own mind. Then, and only then, does it subside and you graduate to your next level.

That ceremony ushered in my new life path. All my suffering, regret, self-contempt, and aimlessness began to dissipate. Among many other takeaways (I cover them in my first book), that ceremony (and more over the years) began teaching me how to withstand severe pressure and stay in the game.

ENDURE

At last, life brightened up after that ceremony in New Mexico and I began a new path. Eventually, I enrolled in a two-year master's degree at Royal Roads University, *while* trying to build my first startup on the side, and *while* working a full-time job. Compared to my previous challenges, this one felt more professional and down to earth. But it wasn't exactly easier.

If the previous two challenges were designed to build your self-awareness and pressure-bearing skills, this third challenge builds your endurance. It answers: Will you stick with something for several years and keep delivering consistent output? Will you stay devoted to your chosen mission? Will you get to the finish line no matter what? With endurance, your answer is yes.

The way to build your endurance is by choosing a special mission and sticking with it no matter what. That means responding to the inevitable boring times with discipline. If you haven't heard of Jocko Willink (ex-Navy SEAL, bestselling author, total badass), I recommend you visit his Instagram and podcast. Notice his motto? "DISCIPLINE EQUALS FREEDOM."

He is spot on. And from my experience, not only does discipline pave the way to freedom, but discipline also equals confidence–true confidence. Once you prove to yourself you can stick with a long mission, it's merely a matter of dusting off your endurance suit for the next mission that presents itself. In your case, it's the long road of building your company.

Before moving on, take a minute to figure out how you'll "conquer your inner bitch," as the famed comedian Joe Rogan loves to say.

Think about the mission you're currently on or want to succeed in. Take an oath (to yourself) that you'll complete it by a certain time. Next, architect a program that carries you to the finish line, no matter what! If you break the oath, that's on you, and I don't recommend that habit. Whenever things get uncomfortable or boring, your mind will start squirming, seeking ways out, and thinking of quitting. That's when you should return to discipline. Endure.

For example, my enrollment into Royal Roads University was the beginning of a two-year marathon that demanded all of my energy. During the day, I performed at my sales job where I needed to win sales every day to impress my bosses and be part of a competitive sales force. During the evening, I worked on my master's program where I wrote academic papers, worked in groups, solved complex problems, and thought critically to get the passing grade. During my "free" time, I invested my own income, effort, and time to grow my startup idea called Pulse Tours from the ground up (a business where I guided people into fully-vetted ayahuasca centers in South America).

I maintained that disciplined program while juggling rent, tuition, bills, relationships, and all the other stuff that life requires from a person. It was grueling, but totally worth it. By 2014, I earned my master's degree and Pulse Tours was attracting customers! I *finally* felt that I had earned my right to pass the jungle of entrepreneurship. But it wasn't only me who felt confident. It was also my father. He had watched me complete my Passage over the years and now felt confident enough to make a small $20,000 bet on me. My next mission? Turn my little "Pulse Tours" income generator into a full-blown company: *Pulse Retreat Center.*

OPERATE WITH PROWESS

Months after that decision, we put shovels to dirt and my stress levels skyrocketed (as expected). Suddenly, I felt the six-week project deadline hanging over my head. Meanwhile, I was relying on at least twenty Peruvian construction workers from a subsistence village in the middle of the Amazon who, on random days, preferred to take the day off. I was struggling like hell, trying to pay everybody on time, barely keeping them motivated, and racing against time so that my prearranged customers wouldn't arrive to a hole in the dirt. In other words, I'd entered the jungle of entrepreneurship.

Now's a great time for your final challenge: you must balance your determination with business intelligence. The difference between irrational danger and adventure often comes down to your level of business prowess. So, I want you maneuvering your business jungle like my old friend Victor navigated the Amazon.

I mentioned Victor briefly in the introduction—he warned me about the importance of carrying a machete in the jungle. He was the one who helped me build Pulse and acted as my jungle guide back in those days. A tough man who understood the Amazon jungle, respected it, and always came out alive with an amazing story. He captured animals—snakes, tarantulas, monkeys, alligators—just by grabbing them off the trees. A real local legend.

One night, during one of my first jungle expeditions with Victor, he showed me just how the jungle can be navigated. He guided my group in a stealth canoe to the lagoon. Soon we saw a pair of eyes glowing red in the darkness. That's when he killed the flashlights. "Watch" he said, steering our canoe toward where he remembered seeing the eyes. Just when he got to arm's length, he thrust his hand in the water and pulled out a live alligator! It was so exhilarating that we made it a weekly ritual at Pulse between ceremonies.

My point is, be like Victor when operating your company. Use intention, prowess, and precision. Above all, *KNOW* the market's labyrinth of risks and consequences. Just as you need a foundation of knowledge before navigating a real jungle, you need a foundation of knowledge before building your business.

To build that foundation, allow the following questions to get you started. By no means are they a thorough representation of what you need to know about business, but it's the least you need:

- **What is your startup endgame?** (your goal one, five, ten years from now)

- **What checkpoints will you hit?** (these checkpoints will become your journey; see Law 5)

- **What are your biggest dangers?** (people, events, or competition that can disrupt or kill your checkpoints)

- **What is your jungle density?** (the general risk profile of your specific market)

- **What gear do you need to thrive?** (the foundational resources to your business)

*(For example answers to these questions, see the **Jungle Prep Questionnaire** in the Appendix.)*

Luckily I studied these questions (and much more) during the two years while earning my master's degree, and it armed me with enough prowess to succeed at building Pulse. Barely.

Six weeks after starting construction, The Pulse Center miraculously opened and we were ready for the first group of customers. In other words: I officially employed twenty locals who depended on me, and I began receiving nonstop bills for loans, food, transportation, taxes, and more. By that point, my small business idea hit puberty and was slamming me with new demands every day. It was a full-time commitment. No turning back.

That is the founder's life. You are responsible for something much bigger than just yourself. A company is a living, breathing organism that will live or die depending on your ability. People depend on it for their life's stability. If your company goes down, they go down. They lose jobs, investments, food, shelter, and sometimes even their marriages. And you are 100 percent accountable.

It's a huge life choice, but it's still a choice I would remake every day. The same reason a boxer enters the ring with another trained killer is why us founders enter the merciless jungle. It's our life's art. Our calling. We don't really have a choice. The jungle is where we belong. Hell, we might even be addicted to the adrenaline of being constantly on our toes.

NEVER FORGET

Without the challenges you just read—and many others—there is no doubt I would've lacked the toughness to grow Pulse Center over the years and, in subsequent years, grow and keep Soltara alive. (I eventually sold Pulse and started my second business adventure by building Soltara.)

Likewise, your company will contain your DNA. How it grows up and impacts the world is a reflection of you. If you never address the weak links in yourself, your business will stay limited. If you crack under pressure, your business will crumble when problems hit. If you aren't disciplined, your company won't last either.

How you complete your Passage is up to you. The key is to earn your right to pass the jungle. Never forget: the jungle doesn't care if you live or die. So always maintain an intimate relationship with struggle. Make love with it. Know it in and out. Because when the jungle declares war on you, you'll need to respond wisely.

Law 2

SHAPE YOUR MIND TO WARFARE

Q1 2020

> *"A true leader has the confidence to stand alone, the courage to make tough decisions, and the compassion to listen to the needs of others. He does not set out to be a leader, but becomes one by the equality of his actions and the integrity of his intent."*
>
> **—General of the Army, Douglas MacArthur**

SOLTARA WAS ALMOST THREE YEARS OLD. FINALLY STANDING strong. Sales at record heights. Several months' worth of retreats sold out. Drawing influencers like 6x Mr. Olympia Dorian Yates, UFC champ Kyle Kingsbury, and the founder of London Real, Brian Rose. As for our advisers? Luminaries in the self-healing sphere like Dennis McKenna and Gabor Mate. All these factors and more began to yield the profits we'd fought two-and-a-half grueling years to achieve. As Soltara's CEO, I could finally relay the news to our investors: "Soltara is blasting on all cylinders; dividends are en route!"

My job was almost done. The startup goal I had set out for in the summer of 2017 was now across the river: business stability. Once we got there, Soltara wouldn't need me to toe the line as CEO anymore. To my imagination, I'd then sign an historic peace treaty with my archnemesis (Failure), smile proudly, and transfer leadership to my cofounder Melissa Stangl. Then I would refocus my efforts on a new business.

After all, creating and building new entities is the lifeblood of the startup entrepreneur. When one painting on the canvas of life is complete, another shall begin. Most entrepreneurs aren't playing this game to manage an already sustainable organization. We need action. We crave growth. We want to win the startup war. Then proceed to another.

Being so close to this goal was why my stomach knotted as my heavy metal bandmate and chief of cuisine at Soltara asked me in January 2020, "Did you hear about this crazy new virus outbreak down in China? They're saying it might be the beginning of the zombie apocalypse." I shook my head. Not because I hadn't heard about it (I had). Nor because I didn't know he was joking around (I did). But because I wanted to shake the question out of my mind. I sensed that the threat of Failure wasn't really gone.

If you read the introduction, you know what unfolded next. Two months later the World Health Organization (WHO) declared a global pandemic. Three months later COVID-19 swept the world, killing hundreds of thousands. The world economy ground to a complete halt. Nations went into immediate lockdown. Borders were sealed. International travel was barred.

An absolute nightmare. How would Soltara service its customers? How would we usher in business stability? How would I pay my employees? These are questions that inundate a founder's mind whenever turbulence strikes. In this case, the answers were obvious: we wouldn't.

And how did I feel watching Soltara plummet from record-high sales, down to zero? It felt like my imaginary peace treaty had been sabotaged. As if my secretary of state had been sitting in the negotiating room with Failure, pen in hand, ready to sign the treaty. It was at that very moment when one of Failure's assassins murdered my secretary of state, fled out the back, and radioed in a bombing raid on our capital city. My war against Failure raged on.

THE WARTIME CEO

Failure is every founder's sworn enemy. The deadliest creature of the jungle. How scary-looking is it? I've seen its face numerous times, smelled its pungent aroma and stanky breath, and I guarantee you it's a snarling, highly creative, haunting presence. It should NOT be underestimated.

Failure has no mercy. It's everywhere and all at once. Lurking in a bush. Waiting at a corner. Planning to launch an air raid on your village from a distance. It has snipers in the bell tower. It stands on the perimeter waiting to ambush you. Sometimes you spot it coming a mile away. Other times it crawls in silently and wraps around you with impossible tightness. It's constantly declaring war on you, calculating, strategizing, and changing its face. One day it's a cash shortage. Another day it's COVID-19.

As haunting as Failure is, you can outsmart it with Law 2.

Law 2: Shape Your Mind to Warfare

You are about to engage the enemy.

If Law 1 showed the tough reality of startup life, Law 2 teaches the psychological approach that wins the war against Failure. Law 2 answers: how are you going to handle the inundation of decisions? How will you counterattack when Failure threatens to ruin your business? What about when your back is against the wall, stress is skyrocketing, and you're wishing life would ease up a little? In these moments, Law 2 is the psychological machete that keeps you safely en route to prosperity.

War should not be taken lightly, however. Especially needless wars. History is marked with monstrous acts, genocides, war crimes, and the list goes on. They can be the playground for evil, and often they are, but if fought for the right reasons, they hold the power to unify a group against a negative force.

Consider all historical wars. Nations are mobilized against the enemy. The face always changes, but the enemy stays the same: failure to win. *Winning* radically governs the nation's every decision, every move, every strategy, and every economic policy. During WWI and WWII, mothers, sisters, daughters, and wives sacrificed their brothers, husbands, fathers, and sons. The war was on the front page of the newspaper. Government and industries radically shifted in order to maximize wherewithal for victory. A laser focus was pointed at one objective: win the war. Founders should learn from this kind of unity and concentration. Your startup must be hyperfocused on conquering Failure. If you shape your mind in this way, all decisions, all actions, and all thoughts will accelerate victory.

If you're like many entrepreneurs, your victory is *Peacetime*. Peacetime is a holy moment. It means you have built a solid brand, solid customer demand, solid team, and solid finances. If you build this fortress, you are far enough from the threat of business Failure to transfer leadership (if you wish). Until that day, your startup needs a CEO with teeth sharp enough to fight. It needs a Wartime CEO.

A Wartime CEO leads from the front by galloping into hard battles with his men, not cowering in the back on his high horse. Think for a moment about George Washington during the American Revolution. Crazy Horse in the Battle of Little Bighorn. Simón Bolívar as he fought for independence in South America. These warriors were revolutionaries. Wartime CEOs are similar in the early stages of a startup. Steve Jobs led Apple. Elon Musk led PayPal, Tesla, and SpaceX. Jeff Bezos led Amazon. With ZERO intention of losing, they led teams through environments of wild unpredictability, serious stakes, and seemingly impossible odds. You can bet they have war stories.

The Wartime CEO can be relieved from duty when the timing is right (for the company and fellow stakeholders). A great example is Aubrey Marcus, the founder of the total human optimization company Onnit. Aubrey built Onnit to a $28Mill company in five short years. Then in 2020 he announced:

> While entrepreneurs can certainly create a lot of value for the world, the goal of any good entrepreneur is to make themselves obsolete so they can extract themselves from the entity. That's what I recently did with Onnit. I created an amazing company, hired the right people to pick up the flag, and now I get to focus on being an indepreneur–podcasts, books, masterminds, courses...all the ways I am meant to serve.[2]

Aubrey realized his strengths and what Onnit needed. However, not everyone wants to be put in that role of leading growth. Some of you reading this might make a better *Peacetime CEO*. If Wartime CEOs are revolutionaries, Peacetime CEOs are optimizers. For example, my cofounder Melissa Stangl is amazingly talented, analytical, intelligent, innovative, and has the empathy to carry Soltara once I'm gone. She would have been the perfect CEO to lead the era we were entering before COVID hit. But Melissa isn't a Wartime CEO...not just yet. So, once it became obvious COVID was waging war against Soltara and our world, I hopped back on my horse.

Before moving to the next section, ask yourself, "Will I be the Wartime CEO my company needs me to be?"

Be honest. Are you ready for tough decisions? Ready for crucial conversations? Ready to bend the rules if duty calls? Ready to lead your company from the front?

OK. Then it is time I explain what the startup war is really made of: decisions. Decisions are the individual moves that advance your startup war. Each decision emits a chain

---

2 Email newsletter from Aubrey Marcus, "Memento Mori: Remember You Will Die," April 17, 2020.

reaction through your organization. And every day, you begin a new chess battle against Failure. Day by day (battle by battle) you will face amazing opportunities, challenging positions, and decisions that cause casualties on both sides. How will you decide?

When COVID struck, it kicked open Soltara's front door. What added to my anxiety was the total uncertainty about the virus. How long would it keep the world in lockdown? How badly would the world be hurt? My team was looking at me for these answers, but I couldn't possibly know, because nobody knew. It's one thing to be in the most important chess battle of your life. It's a different world of pressure when the lights get turned off mid-game.

These next sections shed light on how I made my wartime decisions despite the pressure, and how you should too.

RESPOND, DON'T REACT

On March 16 (the week WHO declared the pandemic) the Costa Rican government closed its borders. It was a nightmare I had to deal with, swiftly. Over the next couple of days, I weighed the evidence and emailed all Soltara investors, clients, and employees: "COVID-19 has spoken. We have no choice but to temporarily suspend operations through April, tentatively reopening May 3."

We canceled six sold-out retreats and stopped accepting new bookings—a tough decision to make on the heels of record sales, but it would have been unethical to accept new customers without evidence that we could safely service them. With zero sales coming in, Soltara's only chance of avoiding bankruptcy was to lay off twelve international contractors and reduce hours for all remaining employees. Heartbroken, we supplied free room and board to employees who were stranded with nowhere else to go.

Would it get worse? Of course! Canceling the retreats left two hundred customers without a retreat *AND* without their $2,500 retreat deposit. Problem was, COVID left many of them jobless and needing their deposit back. Melissa took this especially hard because she feels others' pain very deeply. Her first reaction was to claw money from our reserves and give refunds. I felt horrible too, but as a Wartime CEO, my duty is to understand the magnitude of consequences from every decision. So I went a different route.

Instead of reacting, I responded. *Responding* and *Reacting* are different styles of deciding. Both are triggered by an event (stimuli). It's what happens between the event and reply that makes all the difference.

Responding is based on strategy. The best leaders temper their reply so the stimuli *serves* their desired future. They take space, calculate the pros and cons, and *then* move forward.

Reacting is based on emotionality. In this case, the emotion makes the decision, not you.

Here is the key to responding: *Slow. The. Battle. Down.* Of course, nobody is immune to knee-jerk reactions. From time to time we are all unable to control our reactions. I am no exception. But as much as possible, you should keep cool and look at the battle-field dispassionately. As the old adage goes, "Cool heads prevail."

After slowing the battle, here is what I observed:

Casualties on the left (the case for *giving* a refund): thirty customers on whom COVID is wreaking financial havoc, which I suspected could become worse if the lockdown were extended. For them, life is getting more chaotic with every passing day. That $2,500 retreat deposit would be a lifejacket; giving a refund would help them buy back certainty in their lives.

Casualties on the right (the case for *freezing* refunds): fifteen blue-collar shareholders who invested their retirement pensions, life savings, and inheritance into Soltara; fifteen remaining local staff who relied on Soltara to feed their children and family; ten core international team members who were stranded in Costa Rica with nowhere to go (me, Melissa, Jesse, Matt, Erica, Scott, Silvia, Soi, Francisco, and Maricela); a mort-gage payment that doesn't stop coming. Freezing refunds might help Soltara survive and keep everybody aboard.

In an ideal world, a magic decision could've salvaged both sides. But alas, in the startup war, you are often pitted against irreconcilable routes. Moving left instantly seals off the other route and greatly inconveniences, outrages, or even endan-gers their citizenry. My decision wasn't fun, but after looking calmly at both sides of the equation, I replied to our thirty financially endangered clients by laying down the hard news: "Refunds are impossible right now. Your deposits are good for life. We guarantee you'll be serviced by Soltara as soon as we reopen."

Some understood, some were furious. I couldn't blame them. But my decision was absolutely necessary. If we went left, we would've satisfied the endangered customers but risked Soltara burning to the ground. And if that happened, we'd *never* service anybody again and the rest of those two hundred people who paid deposits (the patient ones, ironically) would end up completely losing them.

That's your job as Wartime CEO. Stay cool and respond. One decision at a time. At first glance, Soltara was surrounded by demanding pressure. No good decision existed. But after observing both sides of the equation, I realized this situation wasn't *really* about satisfying customers. To use the chess analogy, it really came down to either keeping our bishops happy (and thus allowing the rapid death of our king, Soltara) or putting our king in a position to survive (by temporarily dissatisfying some customers). I chose the lesser evil.

STOP MAKING EVERYBODY "HAPPY"

It's important to acknowledge if you made a bad decision or are losing a battle. Staying in the wrong situation can deplete your company's resources and morale. But if you adapt, you can reassemble your power and make a better decision. For example, think back to my previous decision to postpone refunds. The fact that I found myself in that ugly decision *was* a failure—a direct consequence of failing to accumulate a cash surplus. For years leading up to that moment, it had been my goal to build our cash reserves so that we'd *never* be left carrying customer deposits (aka customer debt). But I failed to achieve that before COVID hit.

Along with the rest of the world, I never saw COVID coming. But I did feel *something* coming. Before the pandemic hit, our monthly reports kept showing a massive red flag. I noticed we didn't have enough cash to cover unserviced deposits. That felt dangerous because it meant—in financial language—those deposits didn't count as revenues, but debt! A debt we owed to the customer until the day we serviced them with a retreat!

And *why* didn't we build sufficient cash reserves to cover the debt? If I'm being brutally honest, a big reason was because throughout 2019 we were too scared to make the tough decision to raise retreat prices and to work our employees harder. All because we wanted to keep everybody "happy."

Our logic had been: keep prices inclusive (aka "low") for customers and maintain an easygoing work environment (aka "not very productive"). It was exactly what the plant medicine community loved to see: a picture-perfect healing center, low profits, happy customers, well-paid employees. Everybody happy!

Every time I broached the idea of raising prices and productivity, I started looking like the bad guy in town. I've noticed that this people-pleasing dilemma is especially hard for Peacetime leaders. Because they are so empathic, they never want to disturb the "peace." They want everything in perfect harmony (on the surface). However, while compassion is a keystone characteristic for a CEO, unchecked love can blind the bigger problem. Think of the loving mother who showers her child in adoration, but never lets him know he gained forty pounds this year. That level of unconditional love is admirable, but as the bigger picture gets lost, dangerous consequences go unmonitored.

Remain empathetic and caring while implementing your wartime decision, but never base it solely on making people happy. Not always, but often the optimal decision hurts people's feelings. It might cause stress in somebody's life, make their life more difficult, or put them in an uncomfortable position. You will never lose lives like in a real war, but sometimes the consequences feel just as emotional. So keep a cool head.

I was guilty of keeping everybody happy, until that is, I could no longer turn a blind eye to the red flag on our financial reports. It took me months of fighting internally to increase prices and push our staff toward more productivity. Finally in December 2019, three months before COVID took over the world, I convinced Soltara's management and team. Not everybody was happy, and there were "casualties on both sides," but the optimal decision was clear: we needed a robust balance sheet ASAP.

That one decision was a major reason why we achieved the record-high sales you read about at the start of this chapter. Not only that, but the extra profits helped us build cash reserves at a faster rate. We never made it as far into that initiative as I would've liked, but it gave us enough cash to know I could *possibly* survive COVID. Whereas if we hadn't taken those steps in December—if we kept everybody in their version of happy—Soltara would be dead.

OXYGENATE YOUR MIND

The *ideal* state of decision-making and leading is to be on constant alert. You're constantly scouring the landscape, seizing opportunities, and hunting down Failure. Your mind is like a computer, downloading new inputs, analyzing, deciding—every split millisecond.

But humans aren't robots. We need to sleep, have a drink, make love, forget about our travails for a few hours (or sometimes days). Leadership weighs on you, and its unending alertness can lead to madness if you aren't careful. God knows I'm not perfect. There are days (and weeks) when I can't look at my inbox or Soltara's reports because I am burning out. That's when I click "refresh" on my mind.

As you go about making wartime decisions in your organization, here is the third key: oxygenate your mind! Routinely. Like a soldier who requires rest and recovery to stay fit for active duty, you have to oxygenate your mind to stay psychologically sharp for wartime decisions.

Before progressing to the next section, start building yourself a *reinvigoration ritual*. It will be your greatest ally. Whenever the pressure gets hot, or decisions are weighing down your spirit, use your ritual to get back in warrior mode. Consider these tried-and-true options:

- **A workout regimen** (i.e., medium-weight, cardio and conditioning)

- **Meditation** (i.e., the HeadSpace app)

- **Hot/cold exposure showers** (i.e., thirty-minute sauna sessions or ice baths like the Morozko Forge model)

- **Breathing exercises** (i.e., the Wim Hof method)

- **Yoga** (i.e., Bikram yoga)

- **Nature walks and hikes** (i.e., try finding a serene location or trail near you)

- **Reading or studying breaks** (i.e., a new book or subject that takes you to a special place)

If you are up for the challenge, read *Own The Day, Own Your Life* by Aubrey Marcus and see where it leads you. He lays out a plethora of ways to optimize your life. We all have our unique preferences, so do what actually works for you. I love to hike, do grueling workouts at the gym, spend quality time with my girlfriend, and play heavy metal with bandmates. They all spice up life and calm the jungle in my head. By the time I finish, I usually feel ready to do business with newfound clarity and sometimes breakthroughs.

That's your goal. Avoid burning out. Take well-timed intermissions from the startup jungle. Smell the roses! Trust me, your job as a jungle warrior is going to be much smoother if you keep your thinking abilities as sharp as a katana.

THINK LIKE A GRANDMASTER

Almost one month after the rapid spread of COVID forced us to shut down operations and freeze refunds, the world economy was sealed shut. Costa Rica was saying borders could reopen by May, but deep down I knew it wasn't likely. To me, it was obvious we were no longer operating in jungle daylight. It was nighttime warfare now. Zero visibility. Meanwhile, requests for refunds were still pouring in and my team was pressing me for answers on a multitude of decisions. My head was spinning. *What do I do?* I thought as my mind was plugged into data from various news sources across the internet.

After oxygenating my mind, I sat by myself, thought meticulously about the shifting landscape, and considered all the data, expert opinions, and indicators I could find. Then, and only then, did I reach a firm decision. I announced a company policy which did three things:

1. Drew a line in the sand regarding refunds.

2. Set our tentative reopening date for June 21.

3. Went on to say, "I will revisit this policy on May 4. Until then, no more decisions can be made regarding the matter because COVID is too uncertain."

That decision was twofold. First, it used a firm policy to announce our way forward–a powerful tool for any company. Second, it emphasized the importance of trying to think like a chess grandmaster whenever you are making a fate-defining decision.

That is the final key to wartime decisions: realize deeply that your decisions aren't just about now. Sometimes, you need to make a move for the future. I love Patrick Bet-David's take on this (whom you met in the previous chapter). While on the Rich Dad Radio Show, he explained the different ways chess players design their moves: an OK chess player knows her next one to two moves; a pro knows the next five; a master knows the next ten; a grandmaster knows the next fifteen!

Think about that. The grandmaster sees the fifteenth move! Her fifteenth move is the winning moment she wants! It should be no different for you. Yes, you are at the frontlines. But you can't let yourself get so bogged down by moment-to-moment decisions that you only see two moves. You must keep your eyes to the horizon, watching how the dominoes are *going* to fall, and moving in the direction of a winning attack.

It's why I issued the company policy. You see, the morning Costa Rica closed its borders, I began immediately contemplating my fifteenth move, thinking to myself, *How can I eventually reopen Soltara with a bang?* The policy had calmed the chaos around me so I could finally think proactively on it.

That question started to put things in perspective. It made me realize there were no short-term moves I could make because of the high degree of instability. Airlines were saying they'd begin operating in June, but until I knew flights were coming from our main customer sources (Europe, North America, Australia), how could I bet on it? Also, Peru (where we source ayahuasca medicine from) was beginning to experience widespread carnage from the virus. Everything was indicating an unnavigable landscape and we needed to lay low until jungle daylight returned.

What the policy also did was free up my energy to design a viable "fifteenth move" that *could* reopen Soltara with a bang. My big idea? Earlier in this chapter I mentioned Aubrey Marcus—the inspiring entrepreneur who built Onnit to $28Mill in five years. Well, you should also know that he's a *huge* influencer in ayahuasca space—probably the biggest among the younger crowds seeking self-actualization. He has been featured on Joe Rogan's podcast numerous times and is trusted for only working with the best in the business. So, I thought who better than the legendary Aubrey Marcus to headline the grand reopening of Soltara (if and when COVID ended)? His endorsement and reach could be like flicking on a nitro booster the moment we fire up our engines post-COVID.

My only problem: daydreaming is the easy part. You can imagine a grandmaster move in your mind, but if you can't make it come true, you're left empty-handed. That's why you need Law 3.

Law 3

LEARN TO HUNT

(29 days into lockdown)

> *"I have never worked a day in my life without selling. If I believe in something, I sell it, and I sell it hard."*
>
> —Estée Lauder

I REMEMBER AS A KID, ABOUT ELEVEN YEARS OLD, I LOVED JACK London's book *The Call of the Wild*. It told of miners and trappers dashing off to the Arctic during the Gold Rush. Mesmerized by these adventurers, I made it my goal to catch a rabbit. I wanted to feel as the hunters felt; the total self-reliance of catching my own dinner. So one day I marched into the forest behind my home carrying wire I'd bought from the hardware store. I had no meticulous plans. I just looped the wire and tied it to a tree. Then I waited and dreamed of tasty rabbit stew. I quickly learned it was a naive hunting method. No rabbit was silly enough to wander into my unbaited snare and sacrifice itself for my stew. I walked home empty-handed feeling like Elmer Fudd.

As a kid, this hunting blunder was excusable. My parents kept loving me and cooking dinner. I was still their boy and life went on. But today, as CEO of Soltara, it doesn't work that way. Returning to my village without a successful hunt when it is most needed (aka deals, revenues, new partnerships) is punishable by exile or failure.

Imagine you're the chieftain of a village. Your village respects you as a leader because you have been providing a half-dozen wild boar every month to feed the village. But then, one month, you and your hunters return empty-handed. Your reason? Doesn't matter. Bellies are rumbling. People are getting grumpy. Children are crying. If your losing streak continues, their angst can erupt into a revolution. Some might defect to another village. Or neighboring startups might attack and steal your market share. Suddenly, the board wants you ousted for somebody with the skills to get the job done.

Sound like a fair-weather relationship? Damn right. The unwritten rule about human relationships (especially in business) is nobody wants to be part of something weak. Weakness is a turnoff. And for good reason—in Law 1 you learned that weakness is the jaguar's preferred source of dinner. So, if you cannot hunt at the crucial hours of your startup journey, eventually your village will smell something is not so strong and dependable in their beloved chieftain. The ageless way to maximize your leadership power at all times is by taking Law 3 seriously.

Law 3: Learn to Hunt

Or learn to go hungry.

Hunting (aka selling, influencing, persuading) is a founder's magic power. Elon Musk scores a permit to launch rockets; Joe Rogan brings home a $100Mill deal with Spotify; you (the founder) go hunting and come back with the kill of your desire. Hunting is the art of obtaining what your startup needs to flourish. It's not just about making the sale. It's how you prowl the jungle and return with your village's favorite meat of the month. Maybe that's a mega sale, a legendary partnership, a new round of fundraising, or maybe it's simply selling your newest vision to your organization. They all require hunting: influencing minds in a way that advances your startup's destiny.

Some hate the word "selling." I can't blame them. I too have been wronged by dishonest salespeople over the years. But when I refer to selling, I don't mean taking advantage of people. I mean artfully *influencing* their decision in a way that advances the destiny of *both* parties involved. If used responsibly, this skill is the most positive power in your CEO toolbox. And you will rely on it regularly.

You learned in the last chapter that Soltara found itself amid a world lockdown because of COVID. Since I hate staying idle, I used the downtime to soak in YouTube advice from entrepreneurs like Patrick Bet-David (as you can probably tell by now), Brian Rose, and Grant Cardone. Watching or listening to educational content about entrepreneurship keeps my head in the game and spawns good ideas. Their consensus? They all kept saying that the best entrepreneurs find a way to transform economic downturns into growth opportunities. In other words, while the frightened masses are evacuating the market, the wartime CEO goes hunting for opportunities of a lifetime.

Their advice was a big reason why–during a global lockdown–I went hunting for new opportunities. This time, for two ideas that were more foolproof than rabbit stew.

My first idea was–instead of curling into a fetal position and praying that COVID disappears before bankrupting my company–to get Soltara back on *offense* and shoot for a game-winning touchdown. How? By tracking down investors who want to invest in Soltara's future. Quite the Hail Mary idea, but I knew a cash infusion would empower me to make two grandmaster moves. First, it would give us enough funds to outlast COVID. Second, it would give us enough funds to build a new profit-generating campus at Soltara during our downtime. And that, my friend, would position us to be bigger, faster, and stronger after the pandemic.

In theory. You see, there are no guarantees when hunting. Never. You could do everything right and still come away empty-handed. Scary? Damn right. Especially during something like COVID–the pandemic had many investors clenching their pockets, waiting for things to clear. So, where would I find willing investors? And, what if I didn't? Luckily, I had experienced four successful fundraising hunts in earlier years, and I had learned a few things since hunting as an eleven-year-old. I can't say I felt certain about the idea, but I did feel ready.

The next chapters tell how the idea unfolded. But now, I want to talk about my other idea. In the previous chapter you learned about my idea for a *fifteenth move*: host a legendary retreat with Aubrey Marcus (top influencer in the ayahuasca community, globally respected entrepreneur, and perfect candidate to help reopen Soltara with a bang). Now let me unpack how I inspired Aubrey to say yes.

I won't waste your time with the vast tactics of selling. There are lots to get right: prospecting, presenting, questioning, handling objections, relationship management, appearance, and so on. Mastering this elusive formula can take years of practice, and there are plenty of awesome books and trainers for that. Instead, let's look at the basics that will carry you a long way. For that, let's explore the turning points that led to a mutually beneficial tango with Aubrey.

LEARN FROM "NO"

What I haven't mentioned about the idea is that it really took more than five years to hunt! I began trying to work with Aubrey ever since building the Pulse Center back in 2014. At that time Aubrey was attending Joe Rogan's podcast and talking about his ayahuasca experiences. I was giddy, thinking, *Well, if he values ayahuasca, he'll **definitely** love the experiences we put together at Pulse!* It is worth mentioning that Aubrey had always inspired me. His meteoric success at Onnit, coupled with his enviable playboy lifestyle back in the day, strengthened my belief that I could do big things too. In my mind, it was a partnership of a lifetime—an amazing ayahuasca experience for him and star power for Pulse. So, naturally I invited him to a retreat (free of charge). He responded politely, expressing intrigue in my idea, but ultimately, he never came. I tried furthering his interest numerous times, but to no avail. The years passed by.

The truth about rejections is, no matter how soft-handed they are, they suck. When you put your heart on the line and fall, it hurts. At its worst, a rejection can leave you feeling invalidated. Add in the hours you seemingly wasted trying to sway that person, plus the dashed hopes of a future relationship, and your emotions can turn to anguish. Not much different from being dumped by somebody you *thought* you were going somewhere with.

As founder, you must reconfigure your relationship to "No." Many hunts (depending on your idea, marketplace, and customer) won't succeed. Instead of beating yourself up after a rejection, use it. For example, lions are considered kings of the jungle but only succeed on an average of 20 percent of their attempts to capture and kill prey. How does that onslaught of rejection make them feel? They lick their paws, reenergize, and get hungrier for the next attempt. The quicker you throw yourself into rejection therapy and weaken the sting of rejection (aka Ego), the quicker you start channeling every no into fuel.

This is easier said than done. Some days you are battle weary. It all feels pointless, and your hunt just isn't as exciting anymore. Respect those moments for what they really are: apathy that will pass. Take an intermission; oxygenate your mind like I mentioned in the previous chapter, and get back on the field with newfound inspiration!

I'll never forget the day my father's old-time buddy (a prolific local insurance salesman named Fuzz) said to me, "Dan, if you get a no, all that means is you're not working hard enough." After hearing no hundreds of times in my life (beginning with my first sales job in 2003 selling air purifiers to strangers), I have come to realize that his wisdom is almost always true. If you ever catch yourself wondering why you just heard a string of noes, here is your clue: they *are* the clues. And it is time to get back to the drawing board and decode them.

When do you keep hearing no? Is your offer bulletproof? Was your presentation too unenthusiastic? How can you better remove their pain and replace it with fulfillment? Are you trying to sell somebody who isn't a good prospect? Do you know enough about your prospect?

After enduring a string of kind noes from Aubrey over the years, I finally uncovered the clue. Up until then, my approach had been to convince him Pulse provided the best ayahuasca experience in the world. I was *accidentally* coming across like a product pusher! And I was NEVER going to win with that approach, because he was loyal to a retreat center elsewhere in Peru and wholeheartedly believed they were *crème de la crème*. Plus, Aubrey is an ultrabusy guy. His time is sacred. At his level, it is crucial to judiciously filter opportunities. So, why the hell should he trust me when I say we are the best ayahuasca center?

MAKE IT SAFE

One of the best sales trainers I learned from was Eric Einarson, the brash and roughneck sales manager from the final sales job I had in 2012–2013. During one sales training session, he asked me and my fresh-eyed coworkers this provoking question: "How do you get somebody to trust you?" Next, in big red letters, he wrote the answer on his flip chart:

"BE TRUSTWORTHY!"

How simple! I thought. *Be trustworthy! It made so much sense!* Earning trust is a process, but it flows from actually being trustworthy, honest, caring about your prospect's problem, and watching their back. In short: *make the prospect feel safe to enter your world.* And once they enter, make sure you deliver on your promises! I've come to learn it is the simple yet powerful foundation to all successful (and win-win) hunts.

Trustworthiness is why Soltara even exists. Why did my employees agree to follow me from Pulse to Soltara? Why did my friends and family transfer their life savings into Soltara? What made the local municipality feel safe enough to grant a construction permit? Obviously, there was no silver bullet, but there was a foundation: *my successful track record at Pulse.* Every step of the way, during every presentation, I made sure to emphasize my proven track record, proven market, and proven reputation. I *proved* why I should be trusted. And it unlocked the opportunity of a lifetime.

Remembering this years later, it dawned on me that I never proved my trustworthiness to Aubrey! Without trust, I had been wasting my breath all along! So instead of trying to sway Aubrey, I changed my approach. I invited his colleague, Kyle Kingsbury. Kyle is a retired UFC fighter and active coach for Aubrey's Fit For Service (FFS) program. He is well-acquainted with the other retreat centers in Peru, so I knew he would be able to taste-test the Soltara experience, compare it to other ones, and then report back with an honest verdict to Aubrey. The approach worked— Kyle came with Caitlyn Howe (another FFS coach) and they both loved the Soltara experience! Soon the other FFS coaches visited. First Erick Godsey. Then Whitney Miller, and another Onnit friend, Liv Langdon. All were pleased. Soltara was a hit!

I'd *finally* eliminated the question of *Is this guy from 3,000 miles away trustworthy?* Bingo bango, right? Well, not exactly. Nobody said hunting was a walk in the park. The biggest question still remained unanswered.

ADVANCE THEIR DESTINY

Earlier in this chapter you learned the best entrepreneurs advance while others flee. It's a game-changing habit, but it's not exactly natural. When COVID struck, my natural reaction was to tuck my head down and wait for the storm to pass. But at the same time, I knew if I didn't design a legendary reopening strategy, Soltara would be caught with our pants down and miss a huge opportunity. The time to make it happen was *now*.

Problem was, by the time COVID hit, I was still empty-handed with Aubrey after years of back and forth. Sure, the FFS coaches had loved Soltara, but so? Trustworthiness is foundational, but not enough to entice somebody to fly 3,000 miles and face mother ayahuasca for days. For a long time, I reasoned, *He values ayahuasca!* But ayahuasca itself isn't fun. It is brutal and it severely challenges you. Nobody lives for just that.

What I'm getting at is *value proposition.* Every deal comes to this. Value proposition is what attracts another person to your deal. It answers for the client: "What's in it for me?" "How does this help advance my destiny?" "Why should I say HELL YES! to this idea?"

A bulletproof value proposition is like having gravity on your side—the right person gravitates toward it because it speaks to their deep-rooted desires. How do you build it? Learn more about your prospect; put yourself in their shoes; feel their hurts and wants; and see the world through their eyes.

Ask the question, "If I were them, what would I want?"

Not "If I had their life."

Not "If I were in their position."

More like "If I was THEM, and NOT me, what would I want?"

This magic question opens the door to empathy. The best salespeople have many qualities, but above all is the power to empathize. This question is what finally pulled me into Aubrey's story. As I thought about it, I realized times had changed, and he was no longer *Aubrey the Onnit CEO exploring ayahuasca*. He had entered a new chapter of life. He had stepped down as CEO and devoted his time to speaking and hosting retreats. He was influencing the world in bigger ways. That is what he valued. The proposal of just coming to heal with some friends was no longer as appealing as it once was in the early days.

Armed with this new intel, I completely redesigned my offer and emailed Aubrey again weeks after COVID hit. Here was the gist of the new deal: a week at Soltara, not as a participant, but as a *keynote speaker.* We'd already perfected the keynote speaker program by hosting multiple retreats with Dennis McKenna and Dorian Yates, who'd been coming once or twice a year to host groups who were willing to pay to join the ceremony and authentically bond with one of their heroes.

That offer cracked the code. Aubrey said yes, and we began orchestrating the legendary retreat. Why did he say yes? Because my offer was a crossbreed of two things he treasured most: evolving spiritually *and* helping others to flourish. In other words, it promised to advance his destiny.

PERFECT YOUR WEAPON

Later on, this deal helped us get through COVID by bringing in some nonrefundable upfront deposits for Aubrey's retreat, which helped us weather the lockdown. We'll discuss all that in the following chapters, but in the meantime, I recommend you start perfecting this new secret weapon.

Just as a rabbit would never hop into an unbaited snare, nobody is going to walk into your business and give you a deal without feeling the incentive to do so. Nobody will buy your product, sign a contract, initiate a new partnership, or even pay serious attention to you if they don't know how it will improve their life. Hunting, on the other hand, is about inspiring them with *REAL* life-changing value. The best entrepreneurs can do this in good times and bad times. It's their secret weapon.

To perfect your weapon, you need two things: 1) practice; and 2) great sales trainers. If you aren't in a position to practice, try a sales job. It will teach you the basics in six months. It will also bestow you with a level of self-reliance that stays with you for life (trust me, nothing prepares you for startup life like only spending what you were able to earn in commissions that month). If that idea isn't appealing to you, there are plenty of amazing resources online. Personally, I recommend *Grant Cardone University* or Patrick Bet-David's *The Vault Academy* for the latest sales insights. Even so, nothing beats taking a commission-only sales job and hacking it out through the real-life jungle by yourself.

Whichever method you choose, there is only one question to judge your hunting success: Did you come back with the kill? The signed contract? The sold product? The new partnership? The fundraising round? If so, your tribe will come to respect and trust you over time. If not, then you failed, and you must keep perfecting your secret weapon, because you cannot predict when your startup will need it next.

Law 4

SET YOUR DESTINATION

(39 days into lockdown)

> *"Not all dreamers are winners, but all winners are dreamers."*
>
> —Mark Gorman

BEING THE CEO OF A PLANT MEDICINE COMPANY HAS GIVEN me a unique view into human psychology. I've seen thousands come to Soltara as part of their "vision quest" to find purpose in their life, and then they left with immeasurable excitement for what life has in store for them. When I first experienced the inexplicable magic of ayahuasca in 2010, this appealed only to the intrepid travelers of the world. But now, I'm happy to see all types are waking up to its power—bodybuilders, veterans suffering from PTSD, social media influencers, and of course, CEOs. So why the worldwide change of heart? Personally, I believe it's because of humanity's unstoppable desire to satisfy Law 4:

Law 4: Set Your Destination

Or the jungle will set it for you.

By destination, I mean the Vision of *where* you want your business and life to end up. In the previous chapter you saw the power of hunting. Well, guess what? Your dream destination is what *fuels* your hunts and star performances. Without an unfakable answer to "Where do you want to arrive in one, five, ten, or fifteen years?" your performance degrades into a stale, despairing, "another day, another dollar" experience. Vision, on the other hand, is your X on the map; your Blitzkrieg against Failure; the fission reactor supercharging every thought, decision, hunt, and event along your journey.

It goes even deeper. The Vision that you follow forges you to the version of yourself you ache to become. Everybody has this Higher Self, but it's usually buried under decades of programming, fearful thinking, and denial. Are you made of flesh and bone and human consciousness? Then it's buried down there and screaming for purpose.

Maybe this sounds like a no-brainer to set, but actually most people have no idea what they *really* want out of life, so they never get anywhere meaningful. Instead, they spend their life swirling in the eddies of routine until they wake up one day and realize it's too late to make their mark on the world. That might be acceptable for regular people, but NOT FOR YOU!

As grandmaster of your business and life, setting a destination CANNOT be skipped. Imagine bushwhacking for ten days through a steamy jungle expedition only to discover you traveled in circles! Every "chess move" was a shot in the dark! Every eaten food-reserve was for nothing! Every mosquito-ridden day and blister on your foot was for nothing! Every obstacle you climbed went nowhere! Try explaining that to your hungry employees. Or to yourself.

By now you're probably wondering how exactly to set your Vision, and how to know if it's authentic. If you treat the rest of this chapter like your own "vision quest," it will point the way to your heartfelt purpose: the destination you'll feel *ALL-FUCK-ING-IN* on.

However, I won't show you how to find it from the vantage point of peace and clarity. I'm going to show you how to find it from within the dark place of extreme confusion and uncertainty—from inside the COVID lockdown. After all, we are all bound to feel visionless at times. And if that's you right now, then you're probably freaking out inside, just like I was when COVID blindfolded my business.

BE ALONE

In theory, inking the contract with Aubrey Marcus (the successful hunt from the previous chapter) should have filled me with inspiration. But in reality, I fell into despair. After the excitement of the hunt wore off, I realized how bad my situation was. Not only were my old strategies obsolete, but the likelihood of ultimate business failure was growing by the day. The Costa Rican government *still* had borders shut. Our revenues were *still* turned off. Banks and vendors were *still* asking me for payments. COVID outbreaks were *still* slamming the world. It all seemed so futile that I could hardly move, let alone go hunting for survival funds.

Since all the gyms were closed in San Jose (my usual tactic to clear my mind), I had the insight to leave my apartment and go spend two weeks with my cofounder, Melissa Stangl in Playa Blanca, Puntarenas, where Soltara is located. There wasn't much to do there either, so we kicked back, watched the news, and drank wine together. It felt like a great way to regain certainty in our lives: watch the news to stay updated and drink wine to chill the nerves. Yet it blew up in our faces.

The news did nothing but fill us with volatility. One day they're predicting rainbows: "The stock market is rebounding! A COVID vaccine is on the horizon!" The next day they're predicting an apocalypse: "Plan for the worst depression since the 1930s!"

Melissa and I tried engaging in civilized debates—thinking it was healthier to vent—but it only made things worse. By the end of two weeks, we could barely talk without exploding on each other.

I was feeling even *more* alone now.

Moments like this are counterintuitive. They're the moments when we want to rekindle the good times, to not be alone with our thoughts, and to not face the unbearable doubt in our lives (whatever the reason). So our instinctive reaction is start searching the outside world for what it can't actually give us: clarity.

The correct wartime response is to detach from it all. It feels like the hardest thing to do amid confusion and uncertainty, but nothing gunks up your Vision (and decisions) quite like being attached to distractions and escapes.

Invoking your Vision requires 20/20 clarity. That means having absolutely *nothing* in your periphery. Go on a long hike; spend days in your apartment totally alone; find a café in a new town; take a few grams of mushrooms, and lie under the stars—whatever your favorite technique of being alone is. If you don't have one, marry yourself to one *today* because it'll be your trusty "CEO retreat."

Luckily, over the years I'd worked on my self-awareness enough to realize what I *really* needed was deliberate solitude. Once Melissa and I realized the news cycle had been hijacking our nerves, we came to the only agreement we could: we separated.

I traveled back to Soltara HQ in San Jose; Melissa stayed on the coast. While at HQ, I relied on my dependable technique of spending days *alone* in order to reset my destination.

IMAGINE YOUR FUCK YES! LIFE

After I removed all distractions and escapes from my periphery (including people), I reckoned with the terrifying reality of my situation: Soltara was near death.

If I did nothing, Soltara would go bankrupt in three months. I would have to surrender my apartment in Costa Rica and move to my parents' house in Canada. And I was almost certain that, as a thirty-eight-year-old man, my wonderful relationship with my girlfriend Jimena would crumble. My startup journey would end with me carrying a mountain of debt, four hundred stakeholders who hate my guts, and the stain of failure all over my reputation.

This killed me to be admitting that but it was the medicine I needed to take. A big reason why something like ayahuasca is so transformative is because it *forces* you to face all the gunk that's been impeding your 20/20 vision and get past it.

While in your solitude—your CEO retreat—I recommend getting to the bottom of what is really happening in your life too. Answer with *brutal* honesty. Maybe your life is great. Maybe it's terrifying. The important part is to not escape it. Let the God's-honest-truth pour out of you!

And don't stop there. Make sure you also get to the bottom of *What do I really fucking want from life?*

That question requires more art than science, so feel it out. Explore your mind. Be inspired by wild possibilities. Really imagine yourself living the Fuck Yes! Life of your dreams.

What's it look like?

Make that scene so alive inside of you that the future is already here! Bathe in it, smell it, taste it, sleep with it, and make love to it every night!

If you need help painting that scene with stunning detail, visit the *Fuck Yes! Life Questionnaire* in the Appendix. Spend a whole day filling it out if you must.

Once imagined with awe-inspiring detail, that scene should act like the sun of a magnificent solar system, energizing its surroundings and having an irresistible pull on them. It should be so big, so bright, and so viscerally meaningful that all the heavenly bodies in your personal orbit are attracted to it. Starting with you.

As I confronted these existential questions while in my solitude in San Jose, I began feeling a sort of catharsis. It was as if I had confessed something and was being freed from its heaviness. I've performed this powerful exercise numerous times throughout the years, but each time it starts to reveal something different to me. This time, I felt the spirit of my grandfather, Ian McPherson.

He belonged to a nonprofit conservation called *Men of the Trees* and, living a meager farm life until the age of ninety-six, one of his greatest joys was planting trees on his farm and watching them grow tall over the decades. In the absence of money to pay for anything but used clothing, food for his seven children, and necessities to keep his farm running, he learned to derive joy from seeing his trees grow.

Suddenly, powered by my imagination, I was feeling the same joy. With my face wrinkled, hair white, in my old age, I was standing at Soltara Healing Center and looking at giant Guanacaste trees! The leaves were dancing in the wind and the golden sun had them glowing. By my side, I saw Jimena and our large family. They were smiling, thanking me with their eyes for staying strong throughout the decades and building our Personal Mecca.

That Vision, although simple, reminded me that if I didn't find a way through COVID, then those things would disappear from my destiny. I couldn't let that happen. Soltara might not be EVERYTHING I am going to do with my life, but I damn sure want it to be there for me in my old age. That gave me a special kind of "heart's desire" that beats the shit out of "fear of loss" or "pursuit of wealth" any day of the week.

The only question that remained: how can I make it real outside of my head?

COMMIT TO A MISSION

With your wheels of imagination spinning, you should design a mission that will get you ONE GIANT STEP closer to your Fuck Yes! Life.

Vision is absolutely a prerequisite, but you'll need to get a lot more granular and practical than that as we start to design and execute your destiny. While the Vision of my Personal Mecca gave me the end destination I'm headed to, I still needed to solve the problem of *How the fuck am I going to finance our survival during an indefinite lockdown?* These were the high-level questions I asked myself.

Your Next Mission

- What mission will get you ONE GIANT STEP closer to your Fuck Yes! Life?

- Why is this mission absolutely crucial?

- How will you know when it's a success?

- What is currently holding you back from succeeding?

- What is the name of your mission?

- Who will you need to become in order to complete this mission?

Make this next mission of yours the main motivating factor of your life. It's your Mt. Everest. Your near-term purpose. In the next chapter you'll be designing a strategic route to its top.

In my case, this simple exercise made me realize my old mission of arriving at Peacetime anytime soon was now a mirage thanks to COVID. I had to let that idea go, and urgently design a mission that could attract new investors. If I didn't finance the lockdown period, then we would become insolvent and my Vision would die an ugly death. I also realized that wallowing in misery, drinking wine, and fighting with my cofounder was getting me nowhere, and I needed to pull up my socks and get to work.

I dreamed up "Project Delta." It was a mission I'd been considering for some time: build a second maloca to service more guests on the unused piece of our gorgeous Soltara property. I thought that—just maybe—if I could pitch this new campus idea under the light of optimism to investors, it might be easier to attract new capital than if I was just asking for rescue funds.

If successful, I knew it might be our ticket to the other side of the lockdown. And for me, one giant step closer to my Personal Mecca. My measure of success: hunt enough money to secure the survival and expansion of Soltara.

No matter what.

BECOME LIMITLESS

Remember that the cost of not setting your destination is simply too high. *Especially* in business.

However, nobody can set your destination except you. You can study, read, practice, take useful shortcuts, ask for advice, but at the end of the day, *YOU* are the master of your destiny! *YOU* are the painter of your masterpiece life.

The key is clarity. The more awareness you maintain throughout your life, the better you can set a destination that provides you with limitless motivation.

Law 5

MAP YOUR ROUTE

(48 days into lockdown)

> *"War, or any kind of conflict, is waged and won through strategy. Think of strategy as a series of lines and arrows aimed at a goal: at getting you to a certain point in the world, at helping you to attack a problem in your path, at figuring out how to encircle and destroy your enemy."*
>
> **—Robert Greene,** *33 Strategies of War*

IN LAW 2, I COMPARED COVID TO AN AIR RAID PUMMELING my village. Out of nowhere, Soltara's glory years were destroyed without remorse. Not only that, but once the dust cleared a little, I was hit with the horrifying image: all the carefully crafted strategic routes to our Fuck Yes! Destination had been wiped off the face of the earth forever! Worse, by the time I reset my destination in late May, Soltara was going on three months of lockdown.

In the USA (where most of our customers are from), riots and protests were erupting due to the killing of George Floyd and other unarmed Black Americans. Anyone living through 2020 probably felt like I did—like we were dancing on top of a powder keg inside a wildfire. For our neighboring country, Peru (where we get our ayahuasca), COVID was just beginning to spread like wildfire, pushing their third-world healthcare system to the brink of collapse.

Many of our Peruvian-based Shamans were stranded there, desperately calling me, hoping I could arrange for their safe return to Soltara. But I couldn't. Apparently there were no paths out of this mess. Not for them. Not for anybody. It was a good time for Law 5.

Law 5: Map Your Route

A vision without a strategy will remain a vision and not reality.

In bad and great times, your strategic route is what keeps your business on track to its destination. No strategy? No way of getting there. This is a reality you cannot escape no matter how much you might hate thinking strategically.

Think of strategy as the physics of your business. In physics, every action has an equal and opposite reaction. Likewise, in business, every action will spark a positive *or* negative chain reaction through your mission. Rookie CEOs fail to predict how that chain reaction might unfold. Great CEOs act like "business physicists," fine-tuning their master strategy so every move is emitting a glorious chain reaction.

They do this by staying dynamic, constantly studying the map for openings, and emerging from their "Commander's Tent" with a master strategy no matter what.

Think of the planet-changing example: in the early 2000s, Elon Musk knew that he was up against a ubiquitously unfavorable public perception of electric vehicles. Other inventors had already tried building them in the past at great cost and with limited functionality. Popular car companies had already tried producing them at scale to great failure. The range and performance just weren't there. But really, their master strategy wasn't there.

The wimpy eco-conscious electric car which spoke only to environmentalists was never going to win the war of public opinion. While Elon's ultimate goal *may* have been to produce millions of wimpy eco-conscious electric cars (eventually), he knew he wouldn't get there until he strategically shifted the sea of public opinion to *respect* electric vehicles, first. To shift that sea, he built the most ego-stroking, preposterously high-performing, and expensive sports car he could: the original Tesla Roadster. Once he shattered performance fears with that beauty, he went apeshit on the rest of his master strategy.

Later I'll explore his strategy more, but now, let me show you how I used that same principled approach to retool my own strategy (for Project Delta this time) amid the seemingly hopeless landscape of COVID.

As you read on, swap your bold mission in place of mine. But make sure you have *totally* committed to that mission. Only when you are *ALL-FUCKING-IN* can you observe the chessboard with 20/20 clarity and detect its best openings. Maybe you have heard of the old adage "If there is a will, there is a way." I agree, but I'll take it a step further by saying, "If there is *ALL-FUCK-ING-IN* VISION, there is a route to victory."

CONDUCT COLD-BLOODED SURVEILLANCE

The first thing to know is the jungle chessboard is *constantly* changing. A day just went by? Well, the landscape just got weirder. Made a winning move? Well, Failure countered that move and turned it into a weapon against you. Had a winning strategy yesterday? It might be a loser's strategy tomorrow.

For this reason, ignorance is never bliss. Ignorance always costs you, your employees, and your destiny in the long run. It's the silent, deadly killer of strategy.

Tempted as I was to stick my head in the sand and hope for the best, I needed to fully accept my old routes as dead. Project Delta would be facing a new, albeit more hideous landscape now.

The trick to detecting a victory strategy in any landscape is to observe your chessboard (your landscape and position) **as it is**. You want to be hovering over the chessboard like a cold-blooded spy, not a desperate player fooling himself that everything is OK. If ever you're feeling disoriented by the nonstop action of life or business, use these questions to find the cold hard truth about your mission and way forward.

The Way Forward

- **What is your mission?** Get clear on your mission and make sure you are directing your observations toward that.

- **What is the bad news?** What are the threats facing you or your organization, in order of lethality? Get real. Don't bullshit yourself. You need to see the battlefield in 20/20 vision.

- **What's the good news?** What are your strengths? What "aces in the hole" do you have? Who are your powerful allies? How is your team? What's your cashflow situation like? How is your credit? What season is it in the market?

- **What must happen to reach your destination?** What are the critical one to five moves that must be made to accomplish your mission?

- **What is your Plan A?** Mastermind a Plan A that takes into account the bad news and the good news and can get your mission accomplished.

- **Assumptions?** Think about the factors you assume are given but could hurt if they get taken away.

- **Risks?** What ugly serpents are waiting for you in the bushes? Who's out to get you? What could go wrong? What do you need to keep an eye on? What could take you out completely?

- **Contingencies?** Analyze worst-case scenarios and make preemptive backup plans for potential contingencies and the risks you identified. It's probably not as scary as you think.

- **Next Steps?** Write out your action steps and get to work.

This surveillance will be your eye in the sky, your special intelligence report of what's *really* going on in your mission and jungle. Don't worry about perfecting it. Just write your answers and see where it takes you. The important thing is to build the habit of cold, hard observation. Do this every month until it's part of you.

After observing my landscape by staying plugged into the firehose of information and COVID news, I finally called a meeting with Soltara's shareholders and declared our strategic route forward. Of course, that meeting had to be held over Zoom, where my shareholders and our landlord company (who calls the shots with respect to the property) attended. It lasted two hours, but I'll spare the minutiae since you know much of my surveillance from this story. Facing them, here's the picture I painted of our current chessboard:

> The bad news on the chessboard is our "King" (Soltara) is—just when we were pushing for a promising victory—suddenly in check, and now months away from checkmate (ultimate Failure).

> We are surrounded by fixed expenses ($320K mortgage bill due in November, living expenses for thirty-plus

employees, and more), and our only source of revenue to pay them (ayahuasca ceremonies) has been extinguished indefinitely because of the lockdown.

The good news is we have strong pieces and moves available to us on the chessboard (the grand opening retreat with Aubrey, solid brand, lethal operations and systems, and more), but we **MUST** survive financially until the borders reopen by finding money to pay, especially, for the $320K mortgage payout in November.

To claw ourselves out of this stranglehold, my Plan A is **PROJECT DELTA**: to hunt a $620K investment deal that could pay the $320K AND use the rest to build a new maloca for Soltara during our downtime (this will increase future capacity and revenues, making us stronger after COVID), which is way better than simply borrowing money to stay alive.

I then asked for their vote of confidence on Project Delta and for the $620K.

Understandably, they had mixed reactions. Some (including myself) loved the idea of Project Delta. I was adamant it was the only way to take *total* control of our destiny and possibly bend COVID into the best thing to ever happen to Soltara.

But our conservative investors wanted to wait things out and see how the pandemic would unfold in the weeks to come. Frustrating, but I couldn't blame them. The sum of $620K is no chump change and together we'd *already* poured about $2Mill into Soltara.

Ultimately, the unanimous decision was formed to decline my request for the $620K. I needed to find a different route.

DEFINE STRATEGIC CHECKPOINTS, THEN CRUSH THEM

Once upon a time there was a safe route connecting Colombia and Panama. It was part of the Pan-American Highway which ran from Alaska all the way to Argentina. But those days are long gone. It has since been overtaken by drug traffickers, kidnappers, Marxists, Indians, and jungle wildlife. *The Darién Gap* it's called, and it gives no shortage of ways to die. However, if you are desperate to arrive in North America by unconventional means, the Darién Gap is your only choice by land. You can say that Project Delta was feeling like my Darién Gap: a daunting long shot.

Moments like that are crucial times to map your route. No matter *how* daunting your mission feels, remember that you can skyrocket your chance of success by using the power of reverse-engineering. Just as a GPS calculates a strategic route to your destination (shortest time, or shortest distance, or less traffic, or no tolls), you can design Strategic Checkpoints for your mission.

A Strategic Checkpoint is a time-bound, defined, achievable stepping stone to your destination. The time-bound part is crucial because, in business, time *is* money. The lack of either of those can get you knocked out of the game. So, your goal is never to "get somewhere." Your goal is to "get somewhere specific, by a certain time." This means you must carefully estimate your speed and traffic when picking your checkpoints. Once perfected, your string of Strategic Checkpoints is the highway to your destination.

The master of knowing which Strategic Checkpoints need to be crushed along the way to his destination is Elon Musk, whom I mentioned earlier. Recall how Elon knew that the wimpy, eco-conscious cars weren't going to catch on until the sea of public opinion was shifted regarding electric vehicles. Well, Elon recognized it was a crucial checkpoint and crushed it with the Tesla Roadster. After that, he followed that up with other Strategic Checkpoints that slowly captured market share and started revolutionizing the world standard: the Model S sedan, then the Model X SUV, then the slightly more accessible yet equally high-performing Model 3 compact sedan and Model Y compact SUV, both of which were his endgame production goals—wimpy albeit affordable eco-conscious electric cars. Now, a game-changing, futuristic, electric pickup truck coined *Cybertruck* is slated to be released in 2022. And yes, I put down a deposit on one as soon as I heard the news. I'll probably be the first person in Costa Rica to be seen cruising the beach in this Blade Runner-esque stainless steel beast.

With all the hype of these electric vehicles, and the countless YouTube videos of people playing with their "Ludicrous Mode" speed setting, Tesla established a foothold. Now the real mission is beginning: accelerate the world's transition to sustainable energy. With nearly five Tesla Gigafactories in operation (or being built at the time of this writing), plus meteoric stock prices, plus hundreds of thousands of vehicles produced each year, Elon has proved himself to be a brilliant strategist. And now it's your turn.

I want you to look at the next year of your life and break your Plan A from the previous section into four quarters: Q1 to Q4. Identify three significant Strategic Checkpoints for each of those four quarters of the next year. Use this prompt to define them:

Add those checkpoints into a spreadsheet you can see every single day.

Quarter 1	Quarter 2	Quarter 3	Quarter 4
Checkpoint 1	Checkpoint 1	Checkpoint 1	Checkpoint 1
Checkpoint 2	Checkpoint 2	Checkpoint 2	Checkpoint 2
Checkpoint 3	Checkpoint 3	Checkpoint 3	Checkpoint 3

Attack those checkpoints with extreme prejudice and make sure you're moving toward them every single day. Let them guide your movements. Never let them out of your sight.

There you go. Your destiny is now tied to checkpoints. I have a massive whiteboard outside my bedroom that has my next four quarters' checkpoints listed. Every time I leave or enter my bedroom, I see it. I find it so helpful to see the long game and keep it top of mind, every day. This exercise is also helpful in three-year and five-year timeframes.

Want to check out and relax from life? Then do not become an entrepreneur. If instead you want to become the Indiana Jones of Entrepreneurship like I promised you could in Law 1, it's time you become OBSESSED with crushing your next checkpoint.

Having dinner with your boyfriend or girlfriend? Good. Imagine how crushing that next checkpoint will bring the relationship to new heights! Worried about your parents' health? OK. Imagine how your success will keep them healthy and living a dignified life into old age! Stressing about your 401(k)? Perfect. Fuck your 401(k)! Define strategic checkpoints that will 10X your wealth instead! Struggling to hit the gym? Even better. Build checkpoints into a training program that transforms you into a more lethal entrepreneur (more in Law 9)! Are you walking into the shower right now? Before doing that, laminate your checkpoints and stick them on the shower wall!

You get my point. No matter what you are doing, a voice in the back of your head should be reminding you of your next checkpoint. As a rule of thumb, focus 80 percent of awareness on your next ones and 20 percent of awareness on cold-blooded surveillance. If a disruptive force changes the game on you (aka COVID), switch 100 percent to surveillance, remap your checkpoints accordingly, and then start crushing them again.

After you crush one, celebrate! There is no drug like nailing a goal, nailing it *on time*, and knowing you are abso-fucking-lutely en route to destiny. Savor that feeling because you earned it. Pop champagne! Toast to victory! Then reward yourself with the best gift ever: go apeshit on your next one.

As for my Darién Gap situation (Project Delta), a couple weeks after being declined by our shareholders, I started asking my inner circle if they knew anybody who might be interested in doing the $620K deal. Long shot, but whether I liked it or not, it was my First Strategic Checkpoint on the list. Soltara absolutely needed a cash infusion. Until I got it, my other checkpoints wouldn't see the light of day.

After a few days of beating the bushes, I experienced a wild turn of events. My father managed to track down a possible investor who was mentioned during our Zoom shareholder meeting. Not just any investor. He was also a fellow entrepreneur who happened to be an investor in another healing center in Costa Rica *AND* had recently sold his technology company *AND* because of that was now searching for his next big move *AND* was born and raised in my close-knit hometown of Walkerton, Canada *AND* was somebody who, *somehow*, I never met before! What were the chances that both of us were part of such rare circles, but never crossed paths?

We hit it off big time. We were very aligned as entrepreneurs. We discussed our belief that Costa Rica could become one of the best locations in the world to work with ayahuasca medicine. We agreed that his involvement with the other center here wouldn't be problematic, but rather beneficial to the ultimate goal of putting Costa Rica on the map. We even found out I went to high school with his sister!

We ended our phone call with an agreement to discuss the deal again in a couple days. As you can imagine, I was stoked, feeling like my long shot was happening. On the other hand, I kept that excitement at arm's length. As you just learned: the only reason to pop champagne is when you *crush* a checkpoint. And until I returned to my village with that deal slung over my shoulder, my hunt was not over, and my checkpoint was not complete.

SEIZE THE DAY!

Remember, strategy does not need to be complicated. Don't overthink it! The important part is to honestly look ahead and identify a string of Strategic Checkpoints that will get you to your destination.

Never let strategy become paralyzing. Yes, you want to look ahead and always have a master strategy, but you also need to start moving. Even if you can't see all the way down the field, pick up the ball and start running. Sometimes the path gets clearer as you go further. So grab your pen and paper; write out your Plan A and checkpoints; and start crushing that next one.

Carpe diem!

Law 6

BUILD YOUR MASTERFUL TRIBE

(77 days into lockdown)

"I am not a self-made man. I got a lot of help."

—Arnold Schwarzenegger

OVER THE NEXT COUPLE WEEKS, MELISSA AND I SCOURED THE internet for news about Costa Rica's border reopening. We knew that until we had certainty on Soltara's ability to do business again, the investor who was *potentially* willing to fund Project Delta wouldn't feel comfortable placing the bet on us. But for weeks we found no reliable update on the borders reopening until, in the final week of June, the Health Minister of Costa Rica published a tweet.

It was written in difficult-to-interpret Spanish, so I handed it to my girlfriend for a clear translation and then braced for the news. "This tweet is very confusing," she told me. "But it seems he is saying they won't rehabilitate international tourism until they put measures in place. That's all it says."

I was livid! What was I supposed to tell the investor with that? The Minister's vague tweet offered no date, no reopening procedures, and no expectations for our country to plan their lives around! As a CEO trying to save my company from extinction, I was reminded to never *rely* on outsiders to help you. Soltara was going to ride (or die) based on how seriously I had taken Law 6 thus far.

Law 6: Build Your Masterful Tribe

You are nothing without them.

Your *Masterful Tribe* contains your diehard employees, special alliances, and loyal customers. Together, they form the inner and outer sphere of influence you *can rely on* to propel your bold mission forward. The size and strength of this tribe is like the caliber of a machine gun—and the quantity of bullets—strapped over your shoulder when you roll into battle. Will you show up to the party in a bulletproof APC with a .50 cal mounted on the turret? Or are you carrying a switchblade?

Have you ever read the poem "No Man Is an Island" by John Donne? Well, the title says it all. Regardless of how perfectly you shape your mind to warfare, train yourself to hunt, or strategize your checkpoints, if you are lacking a Masterful Tribe, then you are just another lone jaguar hunting in the jungle, paw-to-mouth. And that strategy has significant limitations.

That is not how you build greatness. Think of Elon Musk or Arnold Schwarzenegger or Oprah Winfrey. From the outside looking in, they are thought to be lone geniuses. But behind closed doors, all of them would confess that they received a lot of help going up the mountain of greatness. They had *serious* horsepower from their inner circles and it helped push them far, fast, and all the way up.

It's why, after the Minister's vague tweet, I found peace in remembering there's a wooden cigar box in my bedroom. Open it and you'll see two different business cards: one card with Melissa's name (my cofounder), and her bloody fingerprint, and the other card with my name and my bloody fingerprint. They are our Blood Oaths.

Melissa and I performed a blood-oath ceremony one night after watching the movie *John Wick 3*. In the movie there is a scene where Wick's old acquaintance hands him a "marker" (a marker is a blood oath which binds your soul to a future request). What happens if you decline the request? Well, go watch the *John Wick* trilogy and thank me later. That scene had my creative juices flowing so much that when we returned to Soltara HQ, I grabbed my knife, pierced my thumb, and pressed blood onto my business card. Melissa followed my lead. From that night on, if either of us wish to cash in that marker and oblige a favor, the other must fulfill their obligation.

Maybe that's extreme. But I believe it's that extreme attitude toward tribe building that has been the backbone to Soltara's growth (pre-COVID). Without the horsepower of a reliable and diehard team, legendary influencers, and loyal fans pushing Soltara uphill over the years, we never would've reached the results that ended up insulating us from immediate bankruptcy. And without them by my side, I am sure the Minister's confusing tweet would've left me feeling like a lone jaguar in an unforgiving jungle.

In Law 11, I'll talk about keeping your tribe satisfied and driven to go to war with you, but in this chapter, allow me to show how to build one first. For that, let's explore the strategies I used to build my Masterful Tribe all throughout the pre-COVID years.

ASSEMBLE YOUR NUCLEAR TRIBE

By the time of the Minister's tweet, Soltara was almost three months into lockdown. That meant my employees were going financially hungry and it wasn't clear when (or if) I'd have the power to change that. Add the fact that we had zero work to keep our minds engaged, and you can see how we started getting cabin fever.

In many other companies this may have caused mass layoffs or resignations. Surprisingly, it deepened the bonds at Soltara. We were suddenly in an unprecedented era together: the leadership team took care of our employees as best we could (paid their rent, air conditioning, laundry, water), the employees volunteered their helping hands around the center, and our landlord even slashed rent by 50 percent to soften our financial pressures. Of course, the dilemma also surfaced uncomfortable conversations that had been festering under the surface, but they needed to be had, and this was a great time for that. On any given night, when we weren't weathering the storm, you could've found us all drinking wine, smoking Mapacho, and howling our tribe motto, *"until the last Mapacho is smoked!"*

That's the spirit of a *nuclear tribe*. Just as a temple is built upon sacred ground and an unbreakable foundation, your company's influence on the world rests upon your nuclear tribe. More than employees, they are like a family—the nucleus of your operation. Close your eyes for a moment and imagine a dartboard. PLEASE DO IT.

See the red bullseye in the middle? That is your nuclear tribe; your indestructible core; your ride-or-dies. Everything flows from there, ripples into all facets of your operation, and then ripples into the world. To generate a stunning ripple effect, you have to pack your nuclear tribe with "A" Players who want more than just a paycheck (if that's the only thing powering your tribe, economic storms will crush your core and your temple comes crumbling down). So, you must hunt down the ride-or-dies who have an unfakable "heart's desire" to play a crucial role in your company's Fuck Yes! Destination.

Their game-time performances over the years will go down in your company's history and earn a permanent seat in your memory. Personally, I can never forget the ones who were screwing in light bulbs and sweeping floors so that I could stall incoming passengers who'd just arrived for our grand opening back in 2018 (in the next chapter, you'll see how down to the wire we were). Or the ones who stuck it out, while others quit when the going got tough. Or the ones who were happy to add a couple extra weeks onto the already jam-packed roster because we were having trouble making payroll (yes, this is a highly common startup dilemma). These moments are just a few examples of how a nuclear tribe helps you crush checkpoints and carry your company over the line to victory!

I know what you're thinking: *Seems great, but how can I locate a lethal pack of ride-or-dies?* When I am not maneuvering the startup jungle, you might overhear thunderous music coming from the guard shack at Soltara's front gate—that's the heavy metal being played by my oldest friend and Soltara chef, Jesse Radford and myself. I tell you this because I believe the glue that keeps any band together, rocking our hearts out, losing track of time, and creating bold music over the years is the same glue which keeps a nuclear tribe powerful: MAGIC.

That magic—a distinct harmony between everybody involved—is so indispensable to your operation that I sat down with Melissa to uncover what causes it. Together, we noticed three *mandatory* traits. As you hunt the next addition to your nuclear tribe, treat the process like an audition and watch closely for the following characteristics.

Are They Masterful?

Like a new bandmate, your candidate should have mastery over his or her individual domain. They will become a vital prong of your company machine, so their unique and complementary talent must plug perfectly into that machine, making it stronger, faster, more appealing to customers.

For example, where would Soltara be without the mastery of our shamans? They are the masters of healing! They have studied plant medicines for decades, and through intense mastery of plant diets, they have become more than intimate with each of the different "plant spirits" they work with. I can't know exactly how they do their healing, but I know they do it at the highest level. As much as our management team keeps Soltara rolling, the real rock stars are these healers, and it ripples into a profound impact on our guests.

Likewise, insist upon the masterful quality in your next candidate. Who's handling your finances? Who's handling your marketing? Who's going to manage your information technology? Look to see if that candidate speaks up and disagrees when it comes to getting things done right. That's a great sign. You need them taking ownership, not shortcuts. And if they aren't masterful yet, make sure they're striving toward it (both in skillset and professional standards).

Are They Loyal?

Loyalty keeps the tribe solid. Hate him or love him, former US President Donald Trump was famous for demanding loyalty from everybody in his orbit. I'm sure this is after having been betrayed in the past and learning how fatal it can be for business (you'll see what I mean in the next chapter). You must feel you can trust tribe members to show up, play strong, and not leave you high and dry just because the going gets tough.

Soltara's head chef, graphic designer, and marketing wizard is Jesse Radford—also a friend of mine for thirty-five years! He is loyal, as masterful as they come, and I absolutely know he's got my back if things get rough. When ideas start flying and stressful disagreements accumulate, there's a natural challenge to hierarchy that tends to happen. The potential for sabotage and usurping is real. You need your own "00" agents watching your back. Jesse runs the kitchen and always has his ear to the ground looking out for me. Sometimes he hears things that I need to know.

Likewise, your candidate should couple their mastery with a high degree of loyalty. They don't have to be from within your network of friends (and they shouldn't be if they are not masterful), but they do need to be predisposed to standing by your side when the kitchen gets hot. Check if your candidate knows how to disagree professionally. Ultimately, loyalty isn't about being 100 percent agreeable. It's infinitely better if they know how to strongly disagree, then hug it out and get back to the mission.

Are They Diverse?

I am not suggesting that you hire unqualified people in order to create diversity for diversity's sake. I am talking about cultivating diversity of life experience and perspective among your tribe. Have you ever felt stuck on a problem until somebody blows your mind with a unique point of view? That is the power of true diversity. A candidate who diversifies the collective consciousness of your tribe will give your startup machine a competitive advantage in the formulation of strategies and decisions.

To meet our diverse family—all the shamans, directors, advisers, and more—you can visit Soltara.co/our-team and enjoy their stories. Reading them will give you a strong sense for what mixing and matching talent looks like. Always be open to welcoming candidates with different personalities, life experience, and backgrounds, because they might shake things up creatively and trigger breakthroughs. But remember: there is a fine line between diversity and disruption. Be diverse where it's wise, but uncompromising about your company's values and mission.

How will you attract your candidates? Easy answer: refer back to Law 3 and hunt them down. In the early days of Soltara, we hunted candidates from our network. After that, we hunted everywhere for them—Facebook, mutual friends, our email list, cold calls, word of mouth.

The key is to know *exactly* who you need and don't settle until you find them. Tribe building, done right, is time-consuming (it took me two years so far), but it's worth agonizing over because you'll be in a long-term relationship with whoever you choose. Like marriage, settling for just anybody will lead to miserable years, friction, and a massive distraction from your company's God-given potential. But if you track down who you need, you will enjoy the rare privilege of navigating the startup jungle with a lethal pack of wolves.

Once you find them, you'll feel confident knowing there is power behind you, ready to pounce at all times. Like when COVID hit and broke my heart as I watched our glory years come to a halt. On the other hand, I was immensely grateful to know I was sitting on a gold mine of talent who couldn't wait to pull off a masterful comeback.

BUILD A POWERFUL ORBIT

In the introduction to this book, you read how I attended the NYC premiere of *ReConnect: The Movie*, a documentary made by the founder of London Real, Brian Rose. The film was touching and inspiring, and I was honored that Soltara shared the big screen in a film that reached hundreds of thousands of people. And, of course, I was happy about the surge in demand that came afterward.

That is the power of building an orbit. If your nuclear tribe sends a powerful ripple through your operation and then the world, your orbit amplifies that ripple into a shockwave. Think of the bullseye again. Can you see the series of concentric circles traveling outward, getting wider and wider and wider? The circle directly outside of that bullseye is your orbit: the carefully chosen alliances you form with luminaries, living legends, and other business allies.

Just like with our involvement in *ReConnect*, sooner or later the orbit you plug into will get you new demand, market access, media exposure, introductions, and so on. Sometimes it's impossible to predict how a new alliance will pay off, but from my experience it eventually does one day. With every new ally, your company accesses a gravity bigger than just yours. It makes both of you more powerful and farther-reaching than you could have been by yourselves.

Luckily, I realized early on that Soltara's emergence as a respected ayahuasca center hinged on our orbit having star power, so I spent serious hours building it. Today we associate with many other living legends, like Dennis McKenna (legendary ethno-pharmacologist devoted to studying psychedelics); Dorian Yates (Google "top bodybuilders of all-time" and stand amazed); Gabor Mate (author of *In the Realm of Hungry Ghosts* and one of the rare physicians talking truth about the link between addiction and childhood trauma).

And of course, Aubrey Marcus, whom you met in Law 3. My alliance with Aubrey over the years has fruited amazing friendships from his inner circle in Austin, Texas, some potent consulting sessions with him, and new market demand for Soltara.

Before you start believing that people like this are out of your league, now is a good time to recall the power of hunting. You'd be amazed at the caliber of orbits you can align with if you keep learning the inner workings of human nature. In Law 3, I explained the first step of hunting is to *make it safe*. Then, you have to offer a way to *advance to their destiny*. This is a simple but powerful one-two punch that, as CEO, you can use in hunts of all sizes. However, when it comes to aligning with strategic orbits, there is a third technique you can use to strengthen your influence: *the law of reciprocity*.

Years ago, in a consulting session with Aubrey, he stressed to me the importance of the law, *Always make sure that your reciprocity account is in balance*. After experiencing massive growth in business and a deep level of inner work over the years, Aubrey had come to the realization that reciprocity is crucial to success anywhere.

What exactly is reciprocity? In short, it's the fact that humans are hardwired to give back. Maybe you've heard the old adage *What have you done for me lately?* That's reciprocity in motion. It's an instinctive reflex that drives human behavior and it will never go away.

Every time you *give* (rather than ask for a favor), you tap the reciprocity reflex in another and make a deposit into your social capital bank with them. With enough social capital built—over time *and* authentically—the other person will naturally want to reciprocate one day. They *want* to include you in new projects. They *want* to help you. They *want* to try your new product.

We all have a social capital bank between our friends, family, and network, but it's invisible and most do not know their existing account balance. Worse, some discover they have a negative balance: social *debt*!

When I founded Soltara, I knew I couldn't waste time building my account slowly because our financial runway was too limited to play the long game. To my mind, the only way Soltara was going to succeed was if I aligned with a powerful orbit in the plant medicine community. I needed fame.

I set my eyes on Dennis McKenna—the esteemed researcher in the psychedelics community and the brother to well-known psychedelics proponent, Terrance McKenna. Nearly every psychedelic diehard knew of Dennis and his late brother. I also knew him from my early days of exploring ayahuasca and admired him tremendously. Problem was, he didn't know me very well.

Linking up with influential people like this can be a catch-22, which you are bound to experience too. The solution is to get your foot in the door with reciprocity. Do that by giving something of *obvious value* to them. This is crucial because people's default reaction to an "ask" is resistance. Especially successful people who are unbelievably busy and get swarmed by asks all the time. Even if they are amazingly kind by nature, they are left no choice but to turn down the onslaught of requests.

So, how did I interest Dennis in working with me? My "give" in early 2017 was to send an email asking Dennis to come on a podcast (my first attempt at running a podcast), which I started growing while still involved with my previous business, Pulse. Although I knew Dennis was generous and probably would have accepted this opportunity to get in front of the community he loved, I also threw in an hourly rate that a doctor might expect to receive.

Dennis accepted my offer and our interview was epic! We discussed all things psychedelics, and by the end of the interview, I felt the beginnings of a new relationship. He also surprised me by saying a big reason he accepted my interview request was because he'd heard amazing things about Pulse and was a big fan of our work. In other words, my nuclear tribe sent a powerful ripple into the world, and Dennis felt it.

Now, here is where many people falter. It is tempting to try extracting value right away. But that isn't how social capital works—that's just an "I scratch your back, you scratch mine" approach, which is severely limited. Like any investment, genuine connections take time to naturally grow. So, after getting your foot in the door, don't ask for anything. Instead, find creative and valuable ways to make further deposits into your social capital account with the other.

I made my second deposit months down the road by offering Dennis another paid interview, which featured him in my first documentary, *The Plant Teacher.* My third deposit was made when—once reciprocity was strongly balanced—I invited Dennis to become a Soltara adviser.

In exchange for his advisory, he would receive a yearly retainer, opportunities to host his own retreats, and unlimited opportunities to speak to the plant medicine community that he loves so dearly. For Soltara, that would magnify our net force of gravity by an order of magnitude, which would attract clients and other allies. Dennis thought this idea was fantastic.

Not long after that advisory pact, Dennis invited Brian Rose to tag along for a retreat. As you know, Brian's experience went on to become the shockwave of *ReConnect*.[3]

ATTRACT TRUE FANS

The shockwave generated by *ReConnect* attracted thousands of new subscribers to Soltara's email list. Although COVID hit before we were able to convert them into retreat guests, we began receiving emails like, "Hang in there! Once you reopen, I'm going to do a retreat! Soltara is more important than ever before!" That moral support and loyalty from our community reminded me why I'm in the game, and that there was pent-up demand relying on our comeback.

This leads me to the third element of your Masterful Tribe: *True Fans*. You can build the most elite nuclear tribe and orbit in the world, but without True Fans, you are playing to an empty stadium. They are the community who believes in your crusade (your business Vision). The first two elements (nuclear tribe and orbit) ripple outward into this community. The more diehard and far-reaching they are, the more sales, success, and staying power you are bound to experience.

---

3 ReConnect: The Movie: londonreal.tv/reconnect-the-movie/.

The idea of true fans comes from the viral article *1,000 True Fans*. In case you haven't read it, here is an excerpt that applies directly to your startup marketing:

> To be a successful creator you don't need millions. You don't need millions of dollars or millions of customers, millions of clients or millions of fans. To make a living as a craftsperson, photographer, musician, designer, author, animator, app maker, entrepreneur, or inventor you need only thousands of true fans. A true fan is defined as a fan that will buy anything you produce...Millions of paying fans is not a realistic goal to shoot for, especially when you are starting out. But a thousand true fans is doable. You might even be able to remember a thousand names. If you added one new true fan per day, it'd only take a few years to gain a thousand.[4]

Congratulations! Now you know Soltara's core approach for attracting loyal customers. Treat that excerpt like your Startup Marketing Playbook. If you can attract one thousand true fans who are obsessed with your product or service (at $1K per fan, let's say) then there is your first $1Mill in revenue! From there, scale up to two thousand true fans. Then three thousand true fans. Then ten thousand. Obviously, there is more to get right with marketing, but true fans are the linchpin. For example, at the time of COVID, Soltara's community was by no means the biggest, but it was authentic, and I'd been growing it since founding Pulse ten years ago. At twenty-eight thousand people strong, I knew it was going to be the launchpad for the comeback I was strategizing with Project Delta.

---

4   1000 True Fans: https://kk.org/thetechnium/1000-true-fans/

To keep your true fans close, the secret is to deliver enriching content, *constantly*. See the pattern? This strategy traces back to Law 3—never stop observing, listening, and learning ways to advance their destiny. Valuable content is music to your fans' ears. They tune in to hear your enriching ideas, stories, and advice. How do you make that music? "Triple down on what you're good at!" as the entrepreneur Gary Vaynerchuk loves to say:

Are you insightful? *Tweet.*

Are you a great writer? *Write articles.*

Are you great on camera? *Start a YouTube channel.*

Are you a brilliant orator? *Start a podcast.*

Are you an exceptionally beautiful specimen of humanity? *Crush it on Instagram.*

Are you loaded with tips and tricks about your expertise? *Become a LinkedIn phenom.*

Just make sure you pick a channel that fans visit a lot. One place that isn't going out of style is email. When I attended the Grant Cardone *10X Growth Conference* during my NYC trip before the COVID spread, a top marketing pro took the stage. Facing thousands of entrepreneurs and hustlers, he delivered a speech that changed how I think about marketing. He explained how online marketing has come full circle. It started with email marketing fifteen years ago. Then it shifted to online search and display ads. Then it shifted again to social media and famous bloggers, and now good ole email is reemerging as the best way to market to people online.

While a new platform like TikTok might possibly implode, or Instagram might lose popularity just like Facebook has, you can always bet on email sticking around. Why? My guess is that in this era of three-millisecond attention spans, people crave something more human and substantial. They don't want a novel, but they do want more than a scroll. Something deeper. Something they can invest in and learn about. It's a major reason why, all throughout the pandemic, I made sure to write emails to our community that were ultratransparent about our lockdown situation, and expressed an appreciative and servicing tone (how I truly felt).

So, whichever platform you pick to reach your True Fans, make sure you eventually direct them to your email signup. It's the most intimate line of communication and it's not going out of style. Oh, and never publish vague tweets to your community. They're not enriching.

BEWARE EGO

My journeys with ayahuasca have played an integral part in maintaining such a high-caliber tribe of rock stars over the years. Ayahuasca has shown me that I'm nothing without my relationships, without my tribe.

Ego might tell you, *You're right and they're wrong! They're stupid and you're smart! You don't need them; you can do it on your own!*

But I've had enough awareness gifted to me by the medicine to temper that urge and pour water on my own flame when it needs to be doused.

In a podcast I later did with Brian Rose, he mentioned that while, yes, we do need to keep our egos in check to maintain harmony in our relationships, "ego is what gets the book done," referring to the value ego does offer. And I agree. Ego wants you to do incredible things so you can be proud of yourself. However, it's tricky and can sabotage your success and your relationships if you untether it and let it run your life.

I highly recommend reading Ryan Holiday's book, *Ego Is the Enemy*. If you have egoic tendencies (like myself and many other entrepreneurs and leaders), you need to drill this into your head. Relationships are really easy to muck up and painfully hard to salvage. And you are NOTHING without them.

Law 7

PLAN FOR SNAKEBITES

(86 days into lockdown)

"He that is not with me is against me."

—Luke 11:23

AFTER READING THAT CONFUSING AND DISCOMFORTING TWEET from the Health Minister, I spent days stewing in my own mental anguish with nothing to do but binge-watch all six seasons of *The Sopranos*, and hope the borders reopened on July 1 (as promised in an older announcement made by Costa Rica's immigration website). But alas, government officials kept our country in suspense until the final days of June only to announce a pushback to August 1! That meant thirty *MORE* days of fighting to keep Soltara alive in a sealed-shut economy—thirty days at least.

Normally I would've digested that news by stepping back, doing surveillance, and restrategizing. But I didn't have that luxury because I was told about another disturbing setback: my girlfriend Jimena's family contracted COVID. In response, police ordered them to remain in total quarantine. If they disobeyed? Well, that would result in fines amounting to three times their

103

monthly income. And possibly jail time. *Fuck this*, I thought, and found myself doing what I had to do. I jumped in my car at 4:00 a.m. and drove for five hours, over the swerving mountains, straight into the rainforest town of Quepos.

There is nothing I despise more than having no control over my own business, my own life, or my own free time with loved ones. To say the least, those back-to-back setbacks (aka snakebites) had me feeling powerless over everything. So, when I arrived in Quepos, I booked a hotel for a few days to regain freedom over my life and administer Law 7:

Law 7: Plan for Snakebites

If you can anticipate the punch, you can block it.

A *snakebite* is any setback (aka lost ground). It can be lost ground with finances, technology, customers, regulators, your tribe, or just one continuously cruel setback like COVID. Setbacks are Failure's favorite attack against the entrepreneur. One by one, they mount pressure, stress, and urgency. The best entrepreneurs treat them as an inextricable part of the jungle.

As the great Sun Tzu wrote in the Art of War, "Don't depend on the enemy not coming, depend rather on being ready for him." Likewise, you should get ready for snakebites because they *NEVER* stop. It took me years to accept that snakebites are simply the cost of doing business. If you enter the business jungle in hopes of avoiding them, you're going to get caught with your pants down.

To show what I mean, look no further than what happened after COVID slammed the world: Brian Rose from London Real was censored by YouTube—an *enormous* setback for his operation. When COVID began picking up steam, Brian started interviewing people who presented perspectives and data that challenged the official narrative laid out by WHO. One of those interviews was with David Icke—a man not shy about calling COVID a conspiracy planned by world governments and the propaganda machine. YouTube didn't agree with the content and heavily censored his channel.

How did Brian respond? Once he felt the pressure from big tech to conform, he built his own censorship-free media platform, *The Digital Freedom Platform.* He raised $1Mill from his loyal community who frankly didn't want to be told what to think by the world's power structures. He went on to host some of the world's most-watched livestreams in history. He *used* the setback to fuel his Vision, kick a dent in the universe, and make his business more invulnerable.

While recovering in my Quepos hotel, I thought of Brian's audacious counterattack. It reminded me how snakebites aren't meant to be fun. If they were, everybody would build a business and thrive. Instead, people usually avoid them like a plague. This leaves you, the entrepreneur, to tame them to your advantage. If you can find a way to thrive on snakebites—even crave them—then you'll be in a league of your own. The greater the sting, the fewer people are willing to be stung.

For the rest of this chapter, I'd like to explore how to handle snakebites by breaking down one bite I got two weeks before driving to Quepos: I was slapped with a $60K lawsuit from an ex-tribe member! Snakebites come from everywhere, but no place hurts more than from your tribe. Think of these sections as the Antivenom I used, and you can too. Without it, any snakebite can kill your business.

WATCH LIKE A HAWK

Like most setbacks in life, that $60K lawsuit had roots in previous years. During the summer of 2017 I met a local Costa Rican named Rico (not his real name) while buying the Soltara property. He was the previous owner's friend and lived on the premises as a beekeeper. I remember taking an instant liking to him because he had a fascinating personality, spoke English and Spanish, and seemed like the perfect candidate to help build Soltara for two reasons.

First, my experience building Pulse in Peru (a landscape similar to Costa Rica) taught me that without a native speaker of the local lingo to help negotiate construction materials and other complexities, I was going to be exploited by the locals who viewed me as nothing more than "a gringo with money." The second reason, according to Costa Rican law, one of our two properties was classified as a "Maritime Zone Property" (meaning it stands within 200 meters of the tideline). According to the law here, all Maritime Zone Properties are required to be 51 percent owned by a local Costa Rican. You can see how I believed Rico was the perfect guy to alleviate both worries. Feeling lucky to find him—and honestly, in need—I welcomed him aboard as my local operations manager and put his signature on the Maritime Zone Property.

Pause. You can probably sense the danger in that decision and how it will start causing me big problems down the road. But the truth is, you're going to have similar moments on your business journey—gut feelings that there is incipient danger. Treat them as reminders that yes, it's true, no matter how great a relationship feels, or how smoothly business is sailing, or how bulletproof your operation appears, a snakebite is on its way. It's just part of the game. Rather than deny it (which causes worse pain), accept it by always occupying two worlds: the world where you smell the roses and seize opportunities (offense), and the world where you watch like a hawk for the snake behind you (defense).

To illustrate why the best entrepreneurs live with a healthy paranoia, put yourself in the shoes of an up-and-coming founder named Joey Mills (not a real person).

Over the past year, Joey crushed checkpoints and scaled his business, SavageMind (not a real biz), which sells natural supplements. It took relentless effort to assemble all the key parts: ten overseas reps; diehard customers; an efficient buying process. Today SavageMind is sustainably earning $10K daily.

Then one Monday morning, while Joey is feeling ecstatic about making his mom and pops proud of him, he checks his inbox and reads a damaging message from the company's payment processor: "Upon auditing your account, we discovered that your business activities don't meet our policy guidelines. We are taking you off-line until you meet our standards. Please contact your account manager if you have questions." With one email,

SavageMind's income is stopped, done, kaput! Now Joey is losing $10K every day this nightmare isn't solved. His customers are getting annoyed, emailing the reps, demanding answers as to why they can't purchase. The reps are forwarding them to him, asking, "What do we do?"

I'd tell Joey to take a breath and acknowledge the real source of his problem: he depended on this snakebite *not* coming. He got swept away while making progress and missed the snake lurking behind him. If he'd kept one eye on defense, he would have had all sorts of opportunities to learn that merchant processors are notoriously annoying to deal with and rewrite policies without notice. A universal business problem. Of course, Joey is a smart guy and he'll learn from this experience. Years ago, a similar setback hit Soltara and inspired us to assign a tribe member as the "hawk" for policy changes and compliance issues having to do with our merchant processors. Joey should plan on doing the same.

This lesson applies to every part of your operation. *Where's the snake?* should always be on your mind. That question is your preventive medicine. In a moment I'll recommend ways to cut down Joey's snake, but for now let's go back to the story that drove this lesson home for me.

Six months after adding Rico to the lease, the construction of Soltara fell into a dire state. Our grand opening was two weeks away, but construction completion was *months* away. Worse, my team was reaching their breaking point and we were down to our final $50K of startup capital. I needed a lifesaver, so I hired a Spanish elite architect named Sandra (not her real name). Her fee was $20K, but I knew she was our only shot. I tasked her to accelerate construction to mach-speed and manage the crew (including Rico). She became our hawk.

Like an Olympic coach, she lit a fire under our ass and demanded excellence. She also knew which dangers to watch for because she'd lived in Costa Rica for twenty years. After a few days of monitoring our operation, she returned to me with a shocking observation about Rico. She said he was overeager to be in the middle of transactions, and whenever he was, he gave preferential treatment to his buddies instead of her vetted contractors. I didn't want to believe this betrayal, but after asking my team about it, they confirmed that Rico had been pocketing a portion of the budget I was giving him—and not in a shy way.

END THE SNAKE

What should you do after learning of a snakebite, and that perhaps it's been biting you the entire time and intends to keep biting until you chop off its head with your machete? First and foremost, take extreme ownership! Don't waste your life by blaming others (even if it is somebody else's fault). Don't indulge in self-pity (even if it is hurtful). Don't expect the problem to fix itself (even if it isn't "your problem"). If you fall into these self-defeatist attitudes, do yourself a favor and read *Extreme Ownership* by Jocko Willink. Anything less than extreme ownership over your life (no matter what's going on) is one hundred times more dangerous than the worst setback. Blame is a slippery slope and leads to nowhere good.

Once you own the problem, the next step is to end the snake. If there is anything my business ventures in Peru and Costa Rica have taught me, it's that you need to act fast! Otherwise, snakes can bite again and their venom travels deep in your business. I recommend the following methods.

Method 1: Hunt the Snake

There aren't many problems that a skilled hunter can't get out of. I wasn't kidding in Law 3 when I said hunting (influence) is a CEO's secret weapon. Sometimes you just need to discover what makes the snake tick, and voilà! With non-people problems like a technical meltdown, you cannot exactly convince it to stop, but you can use the spirit of hunting to move the chess pieces in a creative way. I have lost count of the times I simply talked my way out of problems that looked like they were going to spell my demise.

For Joey's setback (and most all setbacks), the guiding question here is, *How can I influence and relationship-build in order to end this snake?* That question might inspire Joey and his team to call up the merchant processor, get the right person on the phone, convince them that his company will comply with policies moving forward, and that SavageMind wants a strong relationship between both companies. If Joey uses this method accurately, he might be able to resume the company's $10K daily by the end of the week.

Method 2: Manually Fix It

This method is great if you're a bootstrapped business. It entails making use of your human capital (aka the collective brainpower of your tribe) to solve your latest setback.

For Joey's setback, the guiding question here is, *How can I use my team's manpower and brainpower to end the snake?* It might inspire him to go back to the drawing board and find a different solution. If PayPal was the processor that shut Joey down, he can scan the horizon for other providers like Stripe, Transferwise, or Square. This might entail going through hoops, navigating bureaucracy, reviewing documents and policies—much more effort than recovering what he had one day ago, but if he lacks money or a strong relationship with the merchant processor, this could be his strongest option.

Method 3: Use Snakebite Capital

I learned about this method from my mentor, Boyd Willat (a successful entrepreneur from LA who joined me in South America to drink ayahuasca for his seventieth birthday). One day he gave me business advice I never forgot: "Dan, you need Hiccup Capital!" Hiccup Capital was Boyd's terminology for an emergency fund (or as I now call it, Snakebite Capital). He explained that hiccups happen in business, and when they do, money can make many of them go away.

Using the previous example, if Joey cannot recover his account or find an alternate path, he might have to resort to this method. The guiding question is, *How can I use my Snakebite Capital (emergency fund) to end this snake?* By this point, Joey knows the setback is code-red. He might have to dig into his emergency fund, find a talented programmer, offer him a premium wage to quit his job right away and work around the clock to build an in-house payment processor for SavageMind. This is an expensive route—anywhere from $20K to $30K—but losing $10K per day adds up to much worse.

This method came to my rescue numerous times throughout Soltara's existence. So, before reading on, I recommend you start allocating a percentage of your income *just* for snakebite emergencies (the higher your business risk, the higher the percentage). Tom Ellsworth (aka The Biz Doc), one of Patrick Bet-David's closest mentors and a renowned business phenom, told me on a mentorship call that I should have four to six months of expenses stashed in a vault, at all times, only for use in an emergency. When maligned snakes arise, you can often put them to death quickly if you have the Snakebite Capital on hand.

After Sandra's discovery of Rico's betrayal, I spoke to my Chief Financial Officer (CFO). He was already concerned because Rico could never balance his receipts to the budget we set for him. My CFO just assumed Rico was keeping the missing cash as part of his salary, but Rico said that wasn't the case—just that he "lost" the receipts and that we still owed him salary. We tried giving him the benefit of the doubt by keeping a closer eye on his receipts for a few months (while he acted like a bumbling idiot every time we pressed him on it). But the discrepancy piled up. It became obvious he was fucking with us.

Eventually, we pulled Rico aside and offered a generous severance package (Method 3). We agreed to pay him the six months of salary he claimed we owed him, plus a few thousand for random expenses he claimed he used "his own money" for (no receipts, of course). We settled on about $11K.

I hated knowing we were giving him part of our precious startup capital, but it worked. Rico's eyes lit up and we shook hands. He also promised to sign the release of his ownership to the

Maritime Zone Property, and that was to be the end of it. He disappeared.

REMEMBER, IT AIN'T OVER

Problem was, it seemed like Rico believed that he had leverage on us because of his signature on our lease. Emboldened, days later, he returned and asked us to pay for his vehicle to be refurbished! This would cost another $4K, bringing the total up to about $15K! Wanting nothing more than for him to disappear from our lives, we grudgingly shook hands on the $15K under the condition that he sign away his tenure on our Maritime Zone Property and vanish into oblivion.

Instead of returning to relinquish his ownership, days later Rico returned with greater demands. This time touting a letter from the Ministry of Labor saying we owed him more money! In Costa Rica, this is common. Fired employees will go to the Ministry and spin a tale of how poorly they were treated. No questions asked, the Ministry gives them an estimate of how much they can collect from the employer. Rico's was $25K! This time, though, with such a shameless attempt at extorting us, we couldn't even grudgingly accept. We told him to lawyer up and get back to us.

Over the years, Costa Rica's style of governing has frustrated the living hell out of me, but it also taught me a powerful business lesson: setbacks ain't over until they're over.

This equally applies to Joey's "solved" setback. Sure, he's relieved he recovered his $10K daily, but he should know that setbacks can regenerate themselves, respawn from other bushes, or evolve into different kinds of snakes. If he chose Method 3, then his in-house system would require consistent maintenance and management. Over the next year, it could become slow, buggy, prone to losing orders, or crash once a month. If he chose Method 2, his new provider could pull the plug on him just like the old one. If he used Method 1, well, that snake could bite like last time.

Remember that! Unless you abso-fucking-lutely know the snake is finished, it's not. Never let your guard down. Keep your machete raised. Have backup plans. And backup plans to those backup plans.

STRENGTHEN YOUR OPERATION

After I declined Rico's shameless request, a year passed without a word from him. Then, right before I hightailed to Quepos, the snake returned. My lawyer called me saying, "Rico wants $60K now." Turns out Rico spent the year building a case against Soltara. He and his lawyer even found "witnesses" (two ex-employees we fired because they stole from us) and were teaming up against us. My suspicions were finally validated: the whole time Rico was trying to use his "51 percent ownership" to pressure us into paying him an outrageous sum.

But here's what Rico didn't know. While he was scheming, we were fortifying our operation to handle whatever was about to come our way. Back in 2017, after he signed the lease, we took special precaution to include a clause in that contract, allowing our attorneys to transfer ownership anytime. Although Rico was our friend in the beginning, we sensed that he was a risk. So after he started displaying signs of treachery, we swapped off his name and replaced it with a loyal person. For extra precaution, we transferred our property to a different company entity, leaving it two layers removed from Rico's reach.

As for the $60K? My lawyer put me at ease. "We will drag it out for so long that he wishes he didn't do this. And at the end of it, he'll be lucky to get what you had originally settled on." In other words, this wasn't my lawyer's first rodeo. Rico wasn't the first snake he's put to death.

The lesson here is to *use* the setback to strengthen your operation. Using Joey's example, he should let the setback inspire him to strengthen the Achilles heel within his operation. Knowing what he knows now, he can perform a risk analysis on anything that can stand in the way of collecting payments and making customers happy. In that investigation, maybe he detects upcoming legislative changes which are game-changing to compliance. Or maybe he detects upcoming cultural shifts that are going to force merchant processors to change their policies at the drop of a dime. His goal is to walk away from the setback with a stronger business than before the snakebite.

This is what happened at Soltara. Thanks to Rico's treacherous ways, we went on to create ironclad procedures for contracts, payments, and receipts, and we even stopped doing handshake agreements. Look at your next setback with the same logic. Never let your company or lifestyle become so exposed that any one snakebite can kill you. Know where you're at-risk, and then design strategic checkpoints to de-risk you. Maddening as they are, snakebites point to where your operation can be strengthened.

HEAL

In the beginning of this chapter I mentioned that COVID left me at Soltara HQ with nothing to do but watch every episode of *The Sopranos*. As I was watching them, I realized the main character and mafia head, Tony Soprano, is the embodiment of how entrepreneurship can feel. He is *always* dealing with snakebites! He's in a chronic state of decision-making. People turn their backs on him. He gets lonely and even gets panic attacks!

It was a stark reminder that without relief, snakebites can lead to psychological wounds. It's why I said fuck it and drove to Quepos. There I did my version of healing. I blasted my favorite metal music. I called the legendary bodybuilder, Dorian Yates, and we shared our perspectives on the pandemic. I drank Brazilian caipirinhas while watching a troop of squirrel monkeys get in a hilarious fight just meters away from me on the pool deck. In other words, I did what I love! And it gave me peace knowing these were the fruits of my labor.

I tell you this as a reminder to always oxygenate your mind, especially when things are stressful. Eighty percent of the good ideas I've ever experienced came while oxygenating my mind. Whenever snakes are lunging at you, that's when you should *triple down* on the ritual you picked in Law 2. It will help you smell the roses, strengthen your Vision, and drive back over the mountain with inspiration.

Law 8

MASTER YOUR RESOURCES

(96 days into lockdown)

> *"Fighting with perfect economy, you can outlast even the most powerful foe."*
>
> —Robert Greene, *The 33 Strategies Of War*

AFTER I RETURNED FROM QUEPOS, I WAS DONE WAITING FOR the world to change. More obsessed than ever with the comeback of Soltara, I scheduled a call with the investor from my hometown. I needed to know—once and for all—if he wanted to invest in Soltara's future. If not, I was going to look elsewhere. Surprisingly, pretty quickly into our conversation, I heard "Deal!" and the amount we agreed on was $620K to build Project Delta.

It didn't stop there. Our shareholders caught wind of the news and, as I predicted, they had a change of heart regarding their willingness to fund the project. They turned around and asked, "Well, what if **we** supply the $620K instead?" In other words, I went from struggling to hunt a mammoth deal that would save

Soltara, to having the deal slung over my shoulder and another wanting to be picked instead.

How was I feeling? Grateful, but honestly not overjoyed. Great as it was to have resources to initiate Project Delta, I knew that wasn't going to happen unless I *immediately* took Law 8 very seriously:

Law 8: Master Your Resources

Or the jungle will master you.

Law 8 is where a whole new game begins. All your wartime decisions, successful hunts, tribe building, crushed checkpoints, and snakebite survivals will have meant NOTHING if you cannot master your resources. What do I mean by master? I mean guaranteeing that your resources (aka your seed capital, latest round of funding, or monthly income) are converting into abundant profits.

Does the word "profit" make you uncomfortable? I know the feeling. Before I threw myself into the world of entrepreneurship, I hated "this damn capitalist machine!" And now that I'm in the plant medicine community, the word "profit" is taboo here. There are people in our community who think I shouldn't be charging money for ayahuasca retreats. To them, Soltara is just a "western company profiteering off the medicine!"

But I am here to tell you profit is the lifeblood of the organism you call your company. Not five-star reviews. Not hearing

"You have the best company on the planet!!" Not even revenues. Why? Because as intoxicating as it feels to make $1Mill in revenues, or get showered with praise, it only leads to bankruptcy if your expenses surpass revenues month after month. Unless you want that—and it's certainly not what I want—your company must become a profit-generating machine. And the first step is tattooing this formula onto your mind:

Profit = Revenue – Expenses

(P=R–E)

I call that the prosperity formula. Why *prosperity*? Because as entrepreneurs, we don't play this game for comfort. We play to create long-term, bountiful, life-fulfilling prosperity for our village. And in business, there is no stronger indication of prosperity than making ethical *profits*.

The two are inseparable. Got robust profits? Congrats! You can provide yourself and your village with better income, greater benefits, sweeter vacations, and more fulfilling positions! But it all starts with that formula. You must crack the code to everlasting profits.

Thanks to the pandemic, my formula was in shambles. By the time I landed the deal for $620K, COVID had already wiped away $1Mill in revenues from four months of total lockdown. Without getting into the mind-numbing financial details, that translates to: the pandemic shattered three years of progress and rewound our profit situation to where it was at the very beginning! To say the least, I needed to make up for lost time.

The rest of this chapter explores how I guaranteed every cent of that $620K went toward reviving Soltara's profit-generating machine. Not to pre-COVID level. To new and wilder heights. Finances can be a real bitch, but I promise if you do nothing except master these basics, you too will be en route to financial freedom.

ADHERE TO A DISCIPLINED BUDGET

Naturally, I chose to go with our shareholders' offering—rather than the hometown investor's—because they'd been with me since the very beginning. But there was a catch: that $620K was under one condition. Before ponying up the funds, they wanted to see my business plan for the new campus, equipped with budgets as airtight as I could make them. Why? Well, because $620K is a lot of fucking money! Amazing as my track record was with them, how could they *really* know I wouldn't blow their money?

To give you a taste of how life-and-death that question is, imagine yourself in the middle of a ten-day jungle mission, accompanied by four elite tribe members you had chosen to help crush checkpoints. Now, after three days of slashing through a dense jungle, you realize they need food. They are covered with dirt, starving, so thirsty they're sticking out their tongues for raindrops. Then, as you open your bag of jerky rations to give them, you see there's no food left!

No matter how successful of a leader you become, it's painfully easy to run out of resources like that. When you're in the swirl of startup action, resources get depleted in invisible ways. I have faced that desperate moment three times in Soltara's history (and as a result, I needed to stop what I was doing to go on emergency hunts). Trust me, the stress is almost unbearable. The way you avoid it altogether is by getting impeccable at *adhering to a disciplined budget.*

A disciplined budget is a profit-sculpting plan for your company. Like a bodybuilder who adheres to a regimen to become chiseled, the CEO adheres to a budget to make their company powerful, fast, and profitable over the years. And to prove to shareholders you won't accidentally blow their money (or yours) in the heat of action.

My father loves to say, "A budget is a guidepost, not a straight-jacket." So, never allow your budget to make you neurotic. Instead, use it to light the way to profits and prosperity! While there are many kinds of budgets, the CEO's best friend is the Profit/Loss budget (aka the financial statement which reflects your P=R–E situation). It shows you three critical metrics: Revenues (sales you brought in); Expenses (money you spent); Profit (leftover profits).

At the end of every month, meet with your CFO and review your P/L.

Were you on track? Off-track? By how much and why? Did unforeseen expenses eat away at your profits this month? Did you underestimate how much revenue you actually needed? Or, were you a budgeting master and now have abundant leftovers for a holiday party *or* expansion *or* employee bonuses? The more masterful you are at budgeting, the more often you'll find yourself in that last category—and able to attract funds whenever you need them most.

Fortunately, by the time shareholders asked for my budget and plans, I had already spent weeks preparing them meticulously. Once I showed them, it filled them with enough confidence to okay the funds. They *saw* that my plan wasn't a pipe dream. They *saw* that I had a reliable "how" for making that $620K profitable (and one day paying dividends back to them).

Next, I had to actually turn those numbers into reality.

CHISEL UNNECESSARY EXPENSES

> **From**: Daniel Cleland
>
> **Subject**: Staff memo
>
> **To**: Soltara tribe members
>
> This is a bittersweet acknowledgment for me because although I appreciate you all so much more than you could ever know, our financial picture requires us to implement a temporary 25 percent reduction to pre-pandemic salaries across the board.

What you just read is a snippet from the email I sent my team. It hurt to send it. My team is wonderful, loyal, elite. Soltara only exists because of their die-hard commitment. However, after reviewing Soltara's P/L budget, I knew it was necessary.

Think back to the jungle mission from the previous section. Remember that desperate moment of discovering you have no food left for your elite team? Well, my 25 percent reduction—while unpleasant—was our first line of defense against that nightmare situation; it was our "resource diet plan" to keep my troops in lethal condition for the *whole* comeback.

You have hundreds of ways of going on an expense-diet (aka limiting your spending of cash). Payroll just happens to be Soltara's (and most companies') biggest expense. The big idea is, in order for your P=R–E formula to reach its maximum, you have to *chisel away unnecessary expenses.*

Think like a bodybuilder: hyperconscious of what your business consumes every day. Don't become so minimalistic that it sucks the joy out of doing business. Keep that joy, but make sure every single expense is *nourishing* your profit machine.

During tough times, be shrewd. You might have to fire people. You might have to tolerate poor quality desk chairs that are uncomfortable. You might have to negotiate vendor contracts down. Ultimately, it's up to you to discern which expenses are unnecessary. Whatever the decision, hold your ground and expect it to make people uncomfortable in the short term. But remember: it's going to make room for future prosperity (for everybody).

As for Soltara, this shrewdness didn't end with my staff. I asked every vendor to reduce their price by 25 percent; I moved out of the house I was renting and started living in a suite at Soltara; we cut 100 percent of travel costs (obviously); I took an ax to anything that wasn't needed for basic sustenance. All in the name of making room for the Project Delta expenses: new facilitators, healers, security guards, kitchen crews, and the list goes on.

To my pleasant surprise, our team was understanding. They recognized the severity of our financial picture and our need to keep the organism alive for the good of all. They gladly accepted the pay cut and continued their elite and diligent service. Tribe morale had been dampened by the utter uncertainty of the COVID lockdowns, but nobody questioned that we would ultimately pull off the comeback, and everyone was willing to help in any way they could.

UNLEASH YOUR WILDEST REVENUES

By the time I chiseled away those expenses, you should recall that Soltara had already lost $1Mill of revenue from four months of lockdown and that Costa Rican officials had already postponed the border reopening to at least August 1. That meant the earliest Soltara could *really* reopen was on November 1 (because we needed a few months to sell retreats, source ayahuasca, and ramp up for guests). Simply put, we were at risk of four *more* months of zero revenues.

Notice the problem here? No revenues? *Negative* profits! That means your P=R–E formula has sunk into the danger zone, below zero! Instead of accumulating prosperity, your company is piling up IOUs (I Owe You) and eating its own muscle to stay alive.

I say fuck that. As CEO you should have no shame in unleashing your wildest revenues—as long as you make sure you're doing it in a sustainable, predictable, and ethical fashion. Think of your revenues as the bodybuilder thinks about muscle building: even if he adheres to the most pristine diet in the world, that means jack shit if he isn't religiously hitting the weights and producing muscle (aka your revenue). To unleash the wildest revenues and bolster your P=R–E formula, here is what I recommend:

First be like William Heinecke: learn how to "fill a vacuum in your market." There's a special talent for finding a vacuum (an unmet need in the marketplace), but it starts with knowing everything there is to know about your industry. Look for holes and opportunities to sell something innovative that nobody else is offering.

Second, think big and dream big. Think outrageously. Don't let your own limiting beliefs tell you it's not possible; leave that for detailed business analysis. Just start getting your ideas on paper first. You can execute relentlessly later (you'll want the power of Law 10 for that).

Third, make sure your prices are high enough. Don't undersell your company or yourself. Don't be shy. Price it high, and then make sure you overdeliver on your word. A successful business is built by blowing people's minds, one at a time. Then, go back to Law 3 and HUNT, HUNT, HUNT. Sell like your life depends on it...because it does.

Instead of painfully waiting four more months to start producing cash flow, we weighed the data at hand and placed our bet on the Costa Rican government opening up the country by November 1. I knew the Chamber of Tourism was putting heavy pressure on them because the tourism sector (which employs many locals) was hanging by a thread. They would not survive another season closed, and the high season begins in November, so I felt it was probable enough to take the risk. We made the announcement in July:

From: Soltara Healing Center

Subject: Announcing our Grand Reopening!

To: Soltara fans

Here at Soltara, we are entering the heart of the green season, with reminders of nature's abundance, beauty, and resilience all around us. When things seem especially challenging, returning to nature, to our plant allies, to our connection to Earth, have always been our favorite and best tools for dealing with life's ups and downs. For this reason, we are so looking forward to opening our doors again in November.

That email went on to announce Soltara's first ayahuasca retreat since the COVID lockdown in March, and it produced $175K of revenue in three days! Only this time, we made it clear the deposits were nonrefundable in case of COVID disruption. I can't tell you how amazing it felt to unleash all our pent-up demand (from the *ReConnect* documentary too) and be back on track to offering life-changing ayahuasca retreats for the world! Our days of zero revenues were over.

Although I couldn't be sure that COVID wouldn't further spawn into a zombie apocalypse, I made abso-fucking-lutely sure that our revenue turret was locked and loaded. The strategy? Keep announcing legendary retreats, one by one. First, featuring Dorian Yates on November 15 for our grand reopening. Then, Dennis McKenna on December 4. And to start off the New Year with a nuclear bang? The one and only Aubrey Marcus was planning to be our host in January. And oh yeah, our new campus was scheduled to be producing revenues at full blast by the end of 2021.

ACTUALIZE YOUR PROFITS

If you remember one thing from this chapter, make it this: YOUR RESOURCES ARE NOT GIFTS! If you treat them like gifts to be heedlessly consumed by your appetite, you will suffer the same fate of many lottery winners—one year blessed, the next year fatter and broke.

Instead, honor your resources for what they really are: seeds to grow prosperity in this lifetime! The hard part is, unless you love finances (which I do not by nature), disciplined budgeting can be mind-numbing. That's why I believe every CEO should hire a great CFO. While you are in the middle of a jungle mission with your elite team, your CFO will be crunching numbers and—write this down too—*actualizing* your hard-earned profits.

It's not enough to master your revenues and expenses. You must actually *collect* the resulting profits. For example, our $175K was a promising sign, but those revenues were only deposits. And if you recall from Law 2, the global COVID lockdown caused many of our customers to lose their jobs and want their deposits *back*. Who's to say it wouldn't happen again?

That's just one example of how easily profits can disappear. There are hundreds of other ways they slip through the cracks. It's why, even after our CFO made the untimely decision to quit right after the lockdown in March, my father instantly stepped in as temporary CFO. Somebody *always* has to be making sure your profit-generating machine is powerful, dynamic, and most importantly, actually generating profit.

Law 9

SHARPEN YOUR SPEAR

(113 days into lockdown)

"You know how you get to Carnegie Hall, don't ya? Practice."

—Aldo "The Apache" Raine
from the movie *Inglourious Basterds*
(as he carves a swastika into the forehead of a Nazi)

IMAGINE YOURSELF CRAWLING STEALTHILY THROUGH THE jungle: the hunt. You are careful to tread silently. You knew enough to smear pigment on your face and mask your scent with fragrant plants. You made sure to study the animal you hunt: the deer. You learned what it looks like, where it roams, how it behaves. Now you lie camouflaged, waiting for it to cross your path.

Suddenly your ears perk to the faint crunching of underbrush in the distance. Fifty meters away, a glorious twelve-point buck comes into view. He is cautiously tiptoeing forward, scanning the perimeter for threatening movements, inhaling the pungent jungle air through powerful olfactory senses to ensure not even the slightest hint of a predator. Meanwhile you lie dead-stiff, waiting for him to enter your throwing range.

Jackpot. The moment is here; you judge he is close enough to strike. You lunge forward; you launch your spear into the air. Before the deer even knows you launched the spear, it hits a tree six feet away from him. You missed. By a long shot. You *thought* you had him; you *thought* you were prepared, but you weren't. Now the deer is spooked, gone forever, and your village will go hungry tonight—a perfect time to sit in solitude all night, carving Law 9 into your psyche:

Law 9: Sharpen Your Spear

Your life ain't a practice run.

There will be moments in your journey (like with that deer hunt) where you better be holding a *Lethal Spear* (aka a refined toolbox of skills, knowledge, and physical *and* psycho-emotional conditioning). You will be facing endless business opportunities to: forge the partnership of your dreams; have coffee with a juggernaut influencer; and secure funding for the next chapter of your entrepreneurial legacy. All are the same: *one shot* to pierce the flesh of a life-changing opportunity.

A dirty secret about world-class entrepreneurs and performers is they are *not* patient when it comes to staying lethally sharp. Why? Because they understand the game is *always* on the line, and that when a glorious opportunity walks through the door, you don't get a second shot. You get ONE shot. ONE kill. NO exceptions. So, serious performers religiously refine their toolbox. When the time comes to sit at a negotiating table, or go the distance in a championship fight, or pull the trigger on a sniper rifle from a rooftop in enemy territory, they are *already* lethal.

I'll never forget when I attended the 10X Conference in Las Vegas before COVID slammed the world. With thousands of people in the audience, Floyd Mayweather took the stage. Floyd, the undefeated boxer with a perfect 50-0 record. Floyd, the founder of Mayweather Promotions with a net worth of almost $1B. Floyd the articulate fighter turned businessman who was now a few meters in front of me, sharing his wisdom.

After walking around the stage, he sat down to be interviewed by the conference host, Grant Cardone. How did Floyd handle answering questions in front of thousands? Exactly like he goes into a championship fight: calm as an assassin! The man was up there, *knowing* he had a Lethal Spear installed deep into his being. And I am here, telling you the Lethal Entrepreneur is much like Mayweather: prepared for any moment! While the unsharp entrepreneur is flustered by the fear of fucking up, the Lethal Entrepreneur is taking aim.

Who will you be? Don't just say it. Before reading on, actually imagine yourself crossing paths with an opportunity you've been desiring.

What stage do you want to stand on? What guy or gal do you want to encounter? What deal do you want to win? What business or career adventure do you want to grab by the motherfucking horns?

Next, get switched on, *NOW*. Because the way life works is that your opportunity might walk through that door in the next hour! And you must become a Lethal Entrepreneur *before* it does.

For the rest of this chapter, I want to show how to sharpen yourself into that Lethal Entrepreneur. Not using shallow, feel-good motivation, but instead using the same methods which made my spear sharp enough to win the $620K deal. You see, more went into that successful hunt than meets the eye. From the outside, maybe it *looked* easy, but only because my *years* of spear sharpening allowed me to hit the bullseye, naturally.

In your life, there will always be a next level to access. If you use this chapter as the knife to sharpen your lethal capabilities, you'll have no problem diving into it headfirst.

PRACTICE THOUSANDS OF REPS

Would Cameron Hanes miss his shot at a glorious opportunity? Don't bet on it. Have a look at Cam's Instagram and you'll see why. Cam is a professional bowhunter who doesn't let a day go by where he is not taking practice shots (reps) and nailing bullseyes. If he is off by two inches, he missed by a mile. When the opportunity comes to put his arrow through the heart of a skittish bull elk in the mountains of Colorado, you can bet he's taken that shot a thousand times before, and he will nail it dead on.

Be like Cam if you want to evolve into a Lethal Entrepreneur: do practice reps every day. No exceptions. Your goal is by the time you face your golden opportunity, it should *NOT* be the first time! It should be the one-thousandth time your mind, body, and spirit has faced it! So second nature that you feel ice water in your veins.

How does Joe Rogan sit down (twice) with Elon Musk, one of the world's most prolific entrepreneurs, richest men, and smartest people, and absolutely crush a two-hour interview? Because he had done precisely 1,168 and 1,469 interviews beforehand, respectively.

How did Chris Kyle become the most lethal sniper in US military history? Because he never counted on "luck" to carry his bullet across the air and into his target; he counted thousands of practice shots and fine-tuned his supernatural precision.

Need more inspiration? Then follow Cameron Hanes on Instagram. Warning: after a few scrolls you might feel the urge to stretch your capabilities like you never thought possible.

Now it's your turn to uncover ways of practicing. Do you dream of hunting a game-changing deal like Elon Musk does on a consistent basis? Or maybe it's making a crowd lose their breath with laughter at a comedy club like Joe Rogan? Whatever your bullseye is, start small and experiment.

Do one hundred reps on a similar opportunity that is lower risk and easier to do in volume. What went wrong? What went great? What must you change? Unpack these questions after each practice run. Then do one hundred more reps. Slowly but surely your shots will gain precision. One day you are missing the bullseye by six feet; the next day it's five feet; eventually you get closer and closer...and closer until one day the bullseye is effortless.

My $620K hunt is an excellent case study. Why did my shot pierce that momentous opportunity to secure expansion funds? Because I had been practicing for more than fifteen years! All the pieces to that puzzle came together because I had *already* been putting them together for years. I had *already* experienced three emergency hunts in prior years. I had *already* been selling my Vision to the Soltara tribe nonstop. I had *already* done thousands of sales negotiations during my pre-entrepreneurship era. I had *already* been solving problems, negotiating deals, crunching the numbers, and analyzing my finances at Soltara day in and day out. By the time that deal came into my range, it was a matter of throwing that spear one more time.

BECOME A WALKING ENCYCLOPEDIA

When Cam Hanes does practice shots in preparation for a long hunt, do you think he just points and shoots? No. He becomes a walking encyclopedia on ballistics, physics, animal anatomy, equipment specifications, and survival skills for the landscape he's about to enter. When he takes his kill shot, all of that assimilated knowledge in his psyche comes out and skyrockets his chance of success.

That is the power of domain-specific knowledge. It's a weapon itself, the razor-sharp tip of your spear where steel meets flesh. You can practice your throwing mechanics all day long and be able to hit your target, but it's your reservoir of knowledge and direct experiences that make the tip so sharp it kills on contact. It's what gives you a hard-to-replicate *edge*.

When Joe Rogan gets ready to interview one of his legendary guests, does he just wing it, fire up a reefer, sit down to shoot the shit? Or does he also ensure he's up to speed on politics and current events, American culture, and the latest and greatest about his podcast guest? Did Chris Kyle blindly put himself on random Iraqi rooftops? Or did he and his task unit learn about the enemy and their movements, the weapons they used, and where they embedded themselves among the urban war zone of Al-Ramadi?

Take a page from their playbook. Seek new knowledge that can get you closer to a bullseye you want to be hitting. Many entrepreneurs I know read fifty-plus books a year to gain their edge! For example, Ben Greenfield (one of the world's preeminent health and fitness influencers) claims to read one book per day. I suspect by "read" he means "listen on Audible," but that's not the point. The point is you can too! But choose wisely. Not all information will give you a special edge. Choose anything that genuinely calls your attention except garbage entertainment or binging on Netflix.

Personally, I find immense value from devouring personal development content on YouTube, audiobooks, Instagram, and at conferences like the 10X conference. Earlier in this chapter you read how Floyd Mayweather appeared on stage there. But it wasn't just him. There were also legends like Magic Johnson, Usher, Kevin Hart, and John Travolta to name a few. Sometimes nothing beats putting yourself in the orbit of ultrasuccessful people like that. You can *feel* them vibrating with next-level knowledge. Within five minutes, they size you up and say something you didn't see coming and it changes your life forever, like a missing puzzle piece in your life.

Attending that 10X conference weeks before COVID swept the world was, in retrospect, one of the best things I could've done. Every legendary speaker had something in common: they all started from the bottom, kept persisting and pouring heart and soul into their craft until they succeeded. They also warned us to *expect* crushing setbacks along the way, but to rise back up no matter what! When COVID shut down the world, it wasn't clear what I should do, and honestly, I was beginning to get stuck in the quicksand of depression. But their stories sustained my hope throughout the lockdown.

From there, it was a matter of staying plugged into the firehouse of inspiration, news, and other valuable knowledge. As you might remember, I listened routinely to relentless entrepreneurs like Patrick Bet-David (of Valuetainment) and Brian Rose (of London Real) on YouTube. Their shows emboldened me to *hunt* during the pandemic, not crawl into the fetal position and wait for the storm to pass. And where would the $620K deal be without that light-bulb moment?

GET IN PRIME FIGHTER CONDITION

Imagine riding horses, climbing slopes, tracking elk on foot through the bushes, and building your own campfires with Cameron Hanes. How much success would you experience on that hunting trip if you were huffing and puffing the whole time because you hadn't stretched your limits for months? Think you'd be invited again if you were an overweight and lazy slob who couldn't go the distance? No way. You wouldn't even get the chance to point and shoot.

This is why so many prominent entrepreneurs and leaders *insist* on cultivating peak performance. It isn't for shits and giggles. It's because they have *seen* with their own eyes how sloppiness creeps into their life, business, and decision-making whenever they let themselves go. Your mind and body are the machines you've placed in control of your business. Machines need maintenance, upkeep, and attention. If you neglect them, they wear out and eventually break. If those machines break, everything around you crumbles.

The preventive medicine is to get yourself in *Prime Fighter Condition*—the last, but far from least, element of becoming a Lethal Entrepreneur. It's your physical AND psycho-emotional peak power which acts as the explosive force behind your launched spear. It's the condition Mayweather is in, fighting like an assassin for twelve rounds. It's the condition Cam is in, stalking elk for days and nights. It's the condition you—the Lethal Entrepreneur—must reach if you want to absolutely own your uphill business adventure.

How to upgrade to Prime Fighter Condition? This is an area of life where you need to do what works for you, but you've gotta do something.

Does your *physicality* need upgrading so you have explosive energy? Here is a clue that it might: you experience brain fog, confusion, and uncertainty; you sleep in a lot; you have low energy to get through the day; maybe you're a little doughy around the waistline.

If you're in this category, follow people like Aubrey Marcus, Kyle Kingsbury, Ben Greenfield, Joe Rogan, Dave Goggins, or

Cameron Hanes. They all share transformative philosophies, podcasts, or programs designed to transform you into a beast among regulars. Pick whoever suits your style, and then implement relentlessly on their ideas.

Or, does your *psycho-emotional* well-being require upgrading so your Vision, relationships, and pursuits all have clarity and zestful purpose? Clues: Are you your own worst enemy sometimes? Do you sabotage opportunities? Do you get triggered by small stuff, lose your shit, or needlessly explode on people? Do you feel powerlessly addicted to sweets, video games, or drugs?

I was stuck in that headspace for much of my life before 2010, which is why I got involved with ayahuasca and then later built Pulse and Soltara—so seekers like you can tap your inner power and start painting your masterpiece life. You already glimpsed the magic of ayahuasca in Law 1 and Law 4, but if you're still on the fence about psychedelics in general, I recommend reading the GQ article, "From Productivity to Psychedelics: Tim Ferriss Has Changed His Mind About Success." If it still doesn't interest you, cement yourself in meditation, yoga, or other spiritual training—ancient ways of sharpening your ninja-like mind.

I confess, there were times during lockdown where I fell from grace into the quicksand of depression. The pandemic shouldn't have been an excuse, but as humans, we do vacillate. Luckily, ever since I lost sixty pounds one summer as a teenager because I grew tired of being a fat target for bullies, I've maintained a baseline of health which I *never* allowed myself to dip below. And thank God, because it was my lifejacket in the sea of pandemic stress. It kept me lucid, strategic, and energized *enough* to keep hunting when life looked pointless.

As you know, that baseline helped me win the $620K deal. Yet that was *NO* time to switch off and let my spear get dull. In fact, if anything, I knew the enemy Failure was still lurking in the shadows, disguised as COVID, and working harder than ever to defeat me and the world. I knew Soltara's comeback was never going to succeed unless I treated it like Mayweather does his championship fights. So, I made the choice to start treating my health like a full-time profession.

I woke up at 6:00 a.m. every weekday. Then, an uphill hike in the refreshing mountains of Costa Rica, fasted, with nothing in my belly. Afterward, I conducted business duties—mostly strategic moves and keeping the comeback in motion. Come afternoon, you would find me in the gym, crushing a workout and getting hungrier for a nutritious dinner at 6:00 p.m. For the rest of the night, instead of indulgences, I sipped tea while preparing for the next day of my mission.

That choice to treat my health like a job was the same choice you'll face again and again (whether you know it or not). It's the choice to allow your health to fall into a pit and watch your destiny be defeated by life forces, *or* the choice to get into prime fighter condition and become the most lethal entrepreneur possible.

GET SOME

I once read that "luck" is the intersection of opportunity and preparedness, the point where you meet an opportunity and are absolutely prepared to engage and destroy. People will say you were lucky. People will call you an overnight success. People will say you were privileged or had help. But you will know in your heart that you won because–like a soldier who masters himself and his skill–you sharpened your spear to lethal perfection. You won by throwing yourself into experiences, by trial and error, by late nights and early mornings. And you might even have battle scars to prove it.

If not, go get some.

Law 10

THE TIME TO KILL IS NOW

(122 days into lockdown)

"The universe likes speed."

—Joe Vitale

"Whoa..." I blurted. It was May of 2017 and my father was pointing at an opportunity he discovered on his computer. My heart raced; eyes widened; it was pulling on me mysteriously. I started to see the potential.

Crazy thing is, it was a property for sale in Costa Rica, and I hadn't really been interested in buying anything. I'd just sold a majority stake in my first company Pulse and, because of that, I was nursing an identity crisis, clueless as to how to spend my days.

My father, trying to snap me out of my wallowing, proposed, "Well, you built a retreat center in Peru. Why not do it again, but better, in Costa Rica?" Within seconds he had jumped on his computer, typed something in, and was showing me the stunning property he found. "What about this one?"

As you probably guessed, I ended up taking possession of that property and building Soltara around it. To this day, it's staggering to think that my destiny as Soltara's CEO came down to that one *minute*. Had I not known Law 10, I would've blown it:

Law 10: The Time to Kill Is Now

Opportunities disappear without warning.

If Law 9 was about lethal sharpness, Law 10 is about your *Kill Instinct*. In business, a minute of overthinking can mean missing a God-given opportunity. So, when your spear is sharp and the window of opportunity opens, do not overthink it. Do not talk yourself out of it. Just go for the kill, NOW!

Kill Instinct is a mode you must learn to embrace. Obviously, I'm not talking about hurting anybody. I'm talking about that feature in you that overrides all hesitation and pushes for the knockout (the big opportunity, idea, or connection that came through your door). It's always part of you, and it's capable of outrageous possibilities and surprising everybody in the room, even yourself.

The stunning ocean view property on my father's computer triggered that mode in me, instantly. It always comes as the same feeling though: the tinge of nervousness. Never changes. There was a natural tendency to shrink back from the moment— to hesitate–but luckily my years in entrepreneurship had taught me those feelings really mean I'm excited about it, and I should get the ball rolling immediately. It's a simple habit which has single-handedly won me more business opportunities than I can count. Including my destiny.

Now, years later, after hunting the $620K and getting the ball rolling on Soltara's comeback, I started to get that special urge again. I was happy about the comeback, but on the other hand, I realized once we got Project Delta off the ground, it was going to come with a new world of responsibility, strategy, and snake-bites. Personally, I felt that the only way I could handle that new chessboard was if I graduated to the higher echelon of entrepreneurship.

My big idea? Seek mentorship from the one and only, Patrick Bet-David. Recall from the previous chapters that PBD's entrepreneurial insights throughout the pandemic helped me realize I *needed* to hunt more than ever. As you know by now, he is an entrepreneur who inspires me enormously. And, with 2.5+ million followers on one of the premier channels for entrepreneurial thinking, he knows a thing or two about crushing the next echelon of entrepreneurship.

This chapter walks you through how I dusted off the ole Kill Instinct in me again. This time, to seize an opportunity to learn from the best.

ACT WITH URGENCY

Should I wait, or just take my shot? If you ever catch yourself thinking that, just shut up and take the shot. This spirit of *acting with urgency* will win you many opportunities. In my experience, people are more impressed with courage than perfection. You gain respect when you show guts, stand up while others wait, and take your shot. If it turns out to be a bad shot, well, you can always correct course later.

You saw me do this numerous times throughout this book, where I acted before I felt *totally* ready. But when I stop to think about it, the entire painting I call "my life" was made by countless brush-strokes of urgent action. One by one, they garnered me unstoppable momentum toward my destiny, which is what we want.

This advice comes with a warning: be courageous, but never uncalculated or reckless. Sometimes, it is better to bide your time and *not* initiate a future train wreck. Learn how to discern between strategic waiting (waiting for better timing) vs. hesitation (waiting out of fear). The more shots you take, the more you learn.

As an example, I took my shot at requesting PBD to be my mentor as soon as I heard a trusty voice in my head say, *Stop what you're doing, sit down, do it now, don't wait.* It was referring to—once and for all—going onto PatrickBetDavid.com and filling out my application to receive his mentorship, an idea I had been authentically interested in for too long.

One hour after applying, I got the call. On the line was PBD's right-hand man, Jaron, the guy who assesses if candidates are qualified to be mentored.

Before I knew it, forty minutes flew by because we formed an electric rapport. He even told me he watched *ReConnect–The Movie* and heard amazing things about Soltara! By the end of our call, he happily extended an invitation to PBD's next group mentorship call. "It's tomorrow morning, which is why I called you immediately. I absolutely wanted to fit you in. Happen to be interested?"

Whoa! Now imagine if I had waited until tomorrow to apply. Tomorrow **was** the mentorship call! And it would've gone on without me! Without hesitating, I accepted Jaron's invitation, paid the $500 fee, and got that stone rolling.

MEAN IT

At 9:00 a.m. that next morning, I was dressed in a three-piece suit and on a Zoom call with forty other entrepreneurs. After a half hour of orientation, PBD and his team split us into networking groups. Meanwhile, in the background, I saw that PBD was watching for leaders to emerge (or at least that's how I chose to interpret it).

Quickly–but stealthily–I initiated some conversations and did my best to ignite our group's culture. Before long, my group was fired up and exchanging stories. Surprisingly, I noticed that I was the only guy who bothered to dress in a suit. I think PBD noticed too.

Let's dig into what happened there. It happened fast, but it's crucial, even game-defining. If you're going to take a shot at an opportunity, *MEAN IT*! Never half-ass. You don't get points for showing up. You get points for showing up *like a pro*, being locked in, and making things happen.

It would've been easy to dress down and treat the call lightly. After all, there was no dress requirement. But that's not the point. The point is taking your opportunities–your God-given moments–*seriously*. Anything less and people notice.

Think about Soltara. I was once asked why we chose to go with Shipibo healers. The truth is, I never considered anything else. They are simply the best. At Soltara we never just sling ayahuasca; we develop deep reciprocal relationships with the best indigenous healers and international facilitators in the field to serve some of the most powerful medicine available. We show up to deliver, not to just be there. As should you.

Now, back to the PBD call. After the networking quieted down, PBD began answering our questions and soon got around to me. I had spent the night thinking of my question because I didn't want to blow my opportunity. I chose to go with the question that had perplexed me for years leading up to that moment; the one I tried cracking the code to numerous times in the past, but never succeeded at accomplishing: "I am finishing my book manuscript and my objective is to spend the next eight months building a platform for it. What are my next five moves?"

I was expecting a quick response from PBD, but instead he took it to the next level! He pulled up my Instagram and performed an exhaustive breakdown on my current strategy (if there was *anybody* I wanted doing that, it was PBD).

For twenty minutes he guided me, telling me what I needed to get better at, eliminate, and what I needed to crank the heat on if I wanted serious followers. Two hours later, the mentorship call ended. In my hands I had two pages of actionable notes from PBD. As I leaned back in my chair, I realized I had next-level answers to many questions that were beyond my reach twenty-four hours earlier.

High on action, I wasted no time implementing the lessons. I uploaded a picture (of me in my suit, of course) to Instagram that was loaded with the entrepreneurship lessons I just learned on the mentorship call. Of all people, PBD slammed the "like" button.

RELENTLESS EXECUTION

Throughout history, relentless execution has been the deciding factor in countless battles. The surprise attack. The overwhelm. Forcing your enemy to react to your advances rather than give them time to plan their own attacks. Gathering momentum—not losing it no matter what—to become an unstoppable freight train.

In Law 7 (Snakebites), you witnessed how Soltara's construction process fell into a dire state back in 2018. It was a stark business example of how *Relentless Execution* made the difference between the life—or death—of our success. Without those weeks and months of nonstop, brutal execution, we never would've made it over that finish line. And I know this for a fact because we *barely* did. On the day of our grand opening, I ran to the ferry and stalled our guests so that my team could finish screwing in the lightbulbs and sweeping construction dust.

The lesson is that big wins require BIG momentum. Once you've gained a foothold on your opportunity, think like a cage fighter. You wouldn't dare turn your back and walk to the corner *after* infuriating your enemy with a punch. You would've been safer not entering!

Same in business. Do not ease up. Do not stop. Do not slow down. Do not stop until nothing is left on the table. And make that decision only once.

Remembering all this (and what I learned from Aubrey Marcus on the power of reciprocity), I knew I couldn't stop at PBD's group mentorship. I had to make sure PBD was well compensated for his special interest in helping me out. Plus, the group call had given me a taste for my next level, and now I wanted the whole plate.

I reached out to Jaron and told him to lock me in for a lifetime membership to PBD's *The Vault Academy*, as well as a one-on-one mentorship with PBD, for a very healthy price.

That decision was met by harsh criticism from within my village (to some, I shouldn't have been spending that much money on an "unnecessary expense"). But honestly, I didn't care.

My exposure to PBD's bold leadership had already boosted my confidence, authority, and clarity about how I needed to make sure the comeback happened. Now, more than ever, I knew if Soltara failed, it was because *I* failed as its CEO. And I wasn't going to let that happen.

Although my one-on-one with PBD wasn't for a couple months, I had already stepped out of that "old echelon" and I wasn't turning back. From now on, Soltara meant business like never before. And I had to make that known to my village.

FEEL THE RUSH

Remember to move fast and relentlessly enough so that even your colleagues feel a little uncomfortable and can barely keep up. If you have a world-class team and they're feeling uncomfortable with—or shocked by—your speed and relentlessness, it likely means you're moving faster and better than your competition is willing to move.

Don't get me wrong. Much more compassion and mercy are needed in this world. But 2020 has shown that there are hostile forces on this planet and they won't hesitate to annihilate you or your dreams. So, as you pursue your destination, attack your objectives with *extreme hostility*.

From there, magic happens. People in your life sense you are different; that you won't stand by as destiny passes. And powerful orbits *love* supporting something moving fast. They will share their thunder with you. They will root for you. They will latch onto your momentum like it's the last train out.

Law 11

LET THE VILLAGE EAT FIRST

(126 days into lockdown)

"Allegiance, after all, has to work two ways; and one can grow weary of an allegiance which is not reciprocal."

—James Baldwin, *Nobody Knows My Name*

BACK IN 2007, A FULL TEN YEARS BEFORE FOUNDING SOLTARA, I began a year-and-a-half stint with G Adventures, leading groups of travelers overland through a half-dozen countries in Central and South America. G Adventures was my first tour job before it dawned on me to create Pulse Tours, and working there taught me the thorny landscape of the tourism industry. That stint also led me to discovering its hugely inspiring founder, Bruce Poon Tip, who later in 2013 wrote *Looptail: How One Company Changed the World by Reinventing Business*, a book which ignited my entrepreneurial dreaming.

I'll never forget reading the story where he told of being on the verge of bankruptcy, living in a tiny apartment, trying to keep

G Adventures alive, but always making sure to make payroll—*first*—before paying himself! That passage stuck to me because I knew Poon Tip went on to grow G Adventures to hundreds of millions in revenue. So, I filed the story away in my mind for future use.

Soon after reading the book, my professor at the time assigned a final project for my master's degree that I was finishing: "Pick a company and analyze their marketing." Of course, I chose G Adventures. I analyzed their website and spun my findings into a website to promote Pulse Tours (still an idea at the time). The website got me an A, but even better, it became Pulse Tours' primary website and was literally bringing in millions of dollars in revenue until I sold it in 2017.

Reflecting back to that era is a mind trip. Life felt electric, throbbing with possibilities. For the first time in my thirty-two-year-old life, I was legitimately doing this thing called "entrepreneurship." And thanks to ayahuasca, my imagination had taken a quantum leap. I was standing tall, at a precipice, looking forward to a new life, *knowing* that if I imagined my dreams viscerally enough, I could make them come true.

As you know by now, that era cost me my entrepreneurial virginity. And after growing and selling Pulse, it's been hard to pretend that anybody's wildest dreams can't come true if they just learn how to apply the correct attitude and methodology. Even despite the maddening months of COVID, I knew it was all shaping up to be a part of the wild journey that continues to make my life feel like a movie—a movie set in stunning Costa Rica, leading the world's preeminent ayahuasca center, helping others actualize *their* dreams, and then returning home to the lady and life of my dreams. I also cannot pretend that Law 11 deserves most of the credit. Not me.

Law 11: Let the Village Eat First

Good leaders eat last, but that doesn't mean they don't eat best.

Here's a secret that took me years to realize: to make your wildest dreams come true, you have to make lots of other people's dreams come true *first*. I can now take Bruce Poon Tip's story out of my memory file and realize why it stuck to me. When Poon Tip was nearing bankruptcy but *always* making payroll, Law 11 was why. Great leaders like Poon Tip know they won't accomplish anything without a village (aka tribe and community) pushing the company uphill over the mountain. First and foremost, this means you cannot let your ego convince you to get paid first.

The people in your village propel your dreams. *They* are the spinning wheels on your company. *They* donate years of their lives to keep it running, get repaired, and go faster. *They* are suffering long nights by your side to win the startup war. So before filling your own coffers, make sure your village is well-fed (financially and spiritually), dreaming big, and motivated to fight like hell!

If Law 6 taught you to recruit a tribe that is fit for your startup war, Law 11 teaches how to keep that tribe driven. Sure you can build the most masterful tribe in the world, but if you don't keep them driven, well, you can't afford an un-driven tribe! Take my word. Without drive, your village will easily give up or surrender in the business battles you *most* need to win!

A *Driven Village* is your army tank. When fueled sufficiently, they blast through brick walls that would make lesser men and women quit. Obviously, this requires they be fueled by income. But there is also another kind of fuel: the inner fuel they get from knowing they are actualizing their time on earth! If, as their CEO, you find this magical balance, your village won't quit or surrender in the daunting battles. They'll be *ALL-FUCK-ING-IN* and dreaming of ingenious ways to win.

Sound important? Absolutely. But the real question is how will you find this balance in *real* startup conditions? How will you keep your dreams and your village's dreams moving in parallel even in the worst of times?

The COVID pandemic forced me to examine this question in a new light. Even more so after my mentorship call with Patrick Bet-David, which had me feeling like it was 2013 all over again, high on adrenaline, standing at the precipice, and ready to throw myself into a new chapter of life: the rebirth and expansion of Soltara.

If successfully built, operated, and marketed, I knew our campus Project Delta would usher in a fantastic era of prosperity. But now for the *real* startup condition: I hadn't paid my village for months.

That's what I'll explore next. The rest of this chapter shows how I kept my village from turning their back on me throughout the pandemic (six months of no salary) and how I eventually inspired them to march with me into *another* startup war. There are many theories about employee management, but this chapter ain't one of them. This chapter reveals what the jungle has taught me about riding with a Driven Village that Failure cannot destroy.

PROTECT THEIR NEEDS

Think of your village as a living, breathing organism. Many founders make the mistake of believing their village is just a group of separate individuals. While this is technically true, your Masterful Tribe will perform at its peak if it moves harmonically like one intelligent organism.

Your body is a good example. Your goal is to keep that organism alive. First and foremost, you want strong vital organs. If your heart, liver, or lungs become too weak, you could die running up a hill (likewise, if your vital leaders or departments are un-driven or quit and leave you out in the cold, then your organization could expire unless you replace or reinvigorate them). This logic goes straight down the line to the other organs, systems, and functions of the human body. It's not *you* who generates the power. It's *them*!

As founder, your job is to play the orchestra of this organism. Like a conductor, you have to listen intently to your village's spirit, and then wave your wand in a way that keeps it in harmony. How you play depends on your village dynamics, your leadership style, the agreements you made, the current landscape, your destination, and checkpoints. But you must intelligently weigh these factors and arrive at a wise decision to keep the whole organism energized.

Never was this more necessary in my life than when COVID threw my village into an indefinite famine. Recall that by March, revenues came to a screeching halt and payroll (our highest expense) could no longer be met. I suddenly had to make a judgment call about how to keep my village together. I knew I didn't want to fire anybody. I knew I didn't want them suffering. I also knew I didn't want them going AWOL. They were an elite tribe that I carefully assembled through the years, and I knew I would need them more than ever to drive forward a Soltara comeback. Simply put, I couldn't afford to lose them, but I couldn't pay their salaries either.

What was my decision? Now is a good time to talk about a topic dear to my heart: *actualization*.

As you probably noticed, my life's work is devoted to empowering others to self-actualize. Over the years, self-actualization has become a driving purpose in my life. Thing is, I believe it's the secret to maintaining the drive within your village (and yourself). In his book *Eleven Rings*, Phil Jackson (former coach of two unrivaled dynasties: the Chicago Bulls w/Michael Jordan and the LA Lakers w/the late Kobe Bryant) revealed that his coaching style was shaped by Abraham Maslow's research on actualization. Here is how Jackson explained Maslow's discoveries:

> To achieve self-actualization, [Maslow] concluded, you first need to satisfy a series of more basic needs, each building upon the other to form what is commonly referred to as Maslow's pyramid. The bottom layer is made up of physiological urges (hunger, sleep, sex); followed by safety concerns (stability, order); love (belonging); self-esteem (self-respect, recognition); and finally self-actualization.

Maslow concluded that most people fail to reach self-actualization because they get stuck somewhere lower on the pyramid.

Instinctively, I knew this was the key to my decision; I had to protect their pyramids. So, my first move in March was to pause payroll until we could reopen and start accepting bookings again. Alarming to them, but if I let the vital organs die (infrastructure of Soltara), the whole village organism would crumble. This decision would have destroyed their first two layers of their pyramids, but we kept them together by "playing the orchestra" with follow-up decisions.

First, we offered housing at Soltara HQ and the Soltara Center to any of our international contractors and local employees who were stranded in Costa Rica due to the lockdown (eight people including four Shipibo healers from the Amazon). We kept the lights, air conditioning, washing machines, and internet running to make sure it felt as much like home as possible. To protect their sense of freedom and spontaneity, we supplied a car to travel and gas in the tank. Finally, we protected everybody's sense of belonging by ordering shipments of their preferred food two times a week. As for our fifteen local Costa Rican employees, we preserved their salaries at minimal hours and paid their health insurance (luckily nobody contracted COVID). By protecting their needs in these creative ways, we minimized stress levels and energized their pyramids for our six-month shutdown. The best part is we didn't lose anybody.

That's the philosophy. Preserve a Driven Village by becoming a maestro of their needs. Always keep your village organism feeling safe, energized, and moving in harmony. Do it with your own style, but just remember the key: your people enrolled in your village to satisfy their pyramids. They seek a minimum level of safety (financial, psychological, spiritual) from your company. So make sure—especially through challenging times—you're satisfying those needs in an unmistakable way.

But let me be clear. DO NOT become a martyr. Not in the least. Yes, it is your job to protect their drive, but as you learned in Law 2, you can go bankrupt making everybody "their version of happy." Just as there is frivolous spending, there is also frivolous caring. If you resort to pampering people, it will blind you to the hard battles on the horizon. Never forget: you are their Wartime CEO. Always stay grounded in this attitude, because it will clarify the make-or-break battles of your startup war. Iin my case, that was the rebirth and expansion of Soltara.

UNLEASH YOUR BATTLE CRY

Eight chapters ago you already learned what I did after protecting my village's needs. I went hunting for a growth opportunity. As founder, that is your juggling act too: one eye on village drive, the other eye on the company throttle. But like I mentioned in Law 5 (Map Your Route), it's important never to get drunk off wins before reaching the final destination. Here's why: securing my village and landing the $620K investment also meant the new campus was a green light; the point of no return where fabulous new forces would need to be met, and a decisive victory won.

If Soltara was going to open by January 2021 and begin construction on Project Delta, it would thrust us into a new era and double revenues in a few short months. But as never-say-die as I am, I knew that if the COVID lockdown lasted beyond January, it was going to be hard for me to keep Soltara from totally collapsing, along with the new campus crashing down on top of me. Soltara was either going straight to heaven, or down a cliff. And I needed my village *ALL-FUCKING-IN* like never before.

As this book comes to a close, I want you to remember that you will face moments like this in your entrepreneurial journey. Crucial hours. Moments where you are cornered like Bruce Poon Tip in *Looptail*. Battles that can either extend your saga or kill the journey in its tracks. In these special times, you will have to rally your troops to dig deeper, push harder, and think bigger than they knew possible.

Protecting their needs is step one. You cannot rally a village for an arduous battle if they are starving, questioning their involvement, or thinking of another village to join. But once that's nailed, your next step is to unleash your battle cry (your uncompromising declaration of the battle that awaits).

Whatever your next battle is in life or business, your village must know. With absolute clarity, they must visualize a common enemy and promised land. And, the terrifying damage that the enemy won't hesitate to inflict if you don't all band together and execute relentlessly. More importantly, they each must genuinely dream of the glory, be aware of the risks, and voluntarily be *ALL-FUCKING-IN*.

And no, don't expect them to already feel that way. It's always your job to exercise Law 3 and paint the picture of how your company mission will advance their destiny. Show tough love if you must.

My mentorship calls with Patrick Bet-David hammered this point home. He sets an unbreakable tone for how entrepreneurs should lead: just and fair, but assertive and strategic. Now, my time had come.

Determination in my eyes, I called a tribe meeting via Zoom. The day of the meeting, ten tribe members trickled into my Zoom screen. One by one I looked into their eyes, realizing most of them had been to startup war with me. In that moment I felt incredibly honored to be in the presence of such amazing people who were united with Soltara.

"Look at you guys. You're like the fucking Navy SEALs! BY FAR the most capable and competent team in the ayahuasca space. And all top of your class!" I said, the gratitude pouring out of me. Then I got down to business.

I officially declared the *"Rebirth of Soltara."* I let it be known that Soltara wasn't going to survive if we kept acting like a mom-and-pop operation. Soltara had to move on to the next phase of our evolution, or risk dying in an old comfort zone.

That meant saying goodbye to old habits like shying away from profits (a habit which gave COVID the power to be an existential risk to our business). In place of our old ways, we had to grow into something new, bolder, more lethal against Failure, and more transformative for our guests. I stuck a flag in the ground by declaring the *Ten Values and Principles* I believed would be the bedrock to Soltara 2.0's greatness: our new identity.

I then disclosed my plans to step down as CEO. Not immediately, but in a couple years, when the landscape was safer for a Peacetime leader to manage. My goal has always been to grow Soltara to a point where it's being kept alive by the people who helped assemble it, while I focus on the task of bringing new companies into our suite of life-changing experiences. "Once we reach that point, I will hire a replacement," I told them all. Who? Somebody from inside the village who is capable, up to task, and earns it.

Finally, I unveiled Project Delta (the campus expansion mission) in all its glory: the vehicle that would carry Soltara 2.0 to success. I painted the picture of how Delta would increase guests and bookings, thereby accelerating Soltara's comeback, revenues, and profits, as well as kicking open the door to new leadership opportunities for them. But Delta would need people taking serious charge and guaranteeing its success. So, for whoever wanted to commit to leading for the long term, equity in the new project was waiting for them. Soltara's success was their success.

Earlier you learned the secret to living your dreams: make other people's dreams come true first. That's why I unleashed my battle cry *that* way. My goal: raise the stakes and let them pick their own adventure. For the bulls who wanted to run with me, they could take command of new leadership roles and claim a stake in the company. For those who wanted more regularity and easy living, they could stay on the legacy projects at Soltara. And if somebody wanted my job, they could earn it.

There were times in that meeting when I shut up and heard them out. But by and large, it was behind closed doors where I got the real story of how they felt. I held one-on-one meetings with my star players and asked them to their face, "Want to take on more leadership?"

Many vital players literally said, "I'm fucking in!" It turns out they had been dreaming of opportunities like the ones I put on the table. Afterward, I got ready for the ride of my life.

VILLAGE RULES

Is your village weak? You are weak. Is your village strong? You are strong. Those are the rules. The principles you learned in this chapter will keep them well-fed and strong (financially, spiritually, psychologically). But along with these principles, obey these village rules at all times: Never treat them recklessly. Never betray them. Never offend them. Never take advantage of them. And never forget why: without them, your life goes nowhere.

And of course, do not assume they don't have other opportunities. Truth is, talented people always have companies sliding into their LinkedIn messages and trying to recruit them. Your job is to remove any doubt that you are "the one." Income is essential, but it's not about blindly throwing more money at them. It's also about their pyramid of needs, loving the job, and fulfilling their destiny. As the poet Antoine de Saint-Exupéry wrote, "If you want to build a ship, don't drum up the men to gather wood, divide the work, and give orders. Instead, teach them to yearn for the vast and endless sea."

So, always be in touch with their yearnings. Always be listening for clues. Always be inspiring them to take charge as intrapreneurs (entrepreneurial minds who are working inside of your company). If you want to take your people skills to even deeper levels, read *Laws of Human Nature* by Robert Greene and *How To Win Friends and Influence People* by Dale Carnegie. They will make you a master diplomat of your village.

Law 12

PREPARE FOR WINTER

(131 days into lockdown)

> *"Pray for the best, prepare for the worst, and expect the unexpected."*
>
> —Gary Busey

IT FELT LIKE MAGIC TO BE PULLING OFF A COMEBACK. IF YOU told me in February 2020 that COVID was going to shut down the world, debilitate Soltara's operations for six months, and ultimately lose us $1.2Mill in revenue, I would have confessed, "No fucking way we survive." At its worst, the pandemic took me to rock bottom, I doubted my fate, my capability, my every decision. Luckily, I managed—barely at times—to play the Laws well enough to withstand the pressure. And by September, I began seeing signs of COVID's haunting presence retreating over the hills.

Once infection rates began flattening around the world, Costa Rica—true to their word—began allowing flights from twenty states in the USA, plus much of Canada, UK, Europe, and

Australia. That's when, in a take-no-prisoners style, we chose to unveil the arrangement I hunted in Law 3: January's retreat with Aubrey Marcus.

Named *The Road to Realization: One Week Plant Medicine Retreat with Aubrey Marcus*, the retreat sold out instantly to Aubrey's Fit For Service community when he told them of it. That game changer left us officially sold out for November (featuring the one and only Dorian Yates), for December (featuring Dennis McKenna), and now January (featuring Aubrey).

Then in the same week, as if the universe wanted us back with a bang, the *New York Times* published an intense article about ayahuasca's life-changing benefits to PTSD sufferers—and it *heavily* featured Soltara. It was the most high-profile press in Soltara's history, and the local Costa Rican TV channels picked up the story. Much to my entertainment, they were calling Soltara "famous"! I can't deny enjoying the favorable attention.

At last, life was warming up again. After six months of what felt like freezing darkness and near-certain failure, we were officially on-path to our wildest and most profitable year. I was hesitant to call it a full comeback, but I *was* feeling exonerated. Soltara was back, booked solid, driven as hell, and Project Delta was about to make a dent in 2021!

Not just that. I honestly wasn't feeling like the same Daniel Cleland anymore. Having dug deeper than I thought I could have, and having exercised the Laws in ways that surprised me, the experience altered me as an entrepreneur. I've always believed we each possess a *"ness"*—a golden quality, style, and energy that makes you **YOU**–and by this point in the story, you can say my "Dan*ness*" was plugged into an amplifier.

The reason: from inside the six-month lockdown, I had glimpsed a hidden dimension to entrepreneurship. One that illuminated the wasteful nature of pussyfooting around or holding back on my leadership instincts whatsoever. As you observed, this journey had a razor-thin margin for error. *One* knee-jerk decision, *one* hesitation, *one* failure to implement any of the Laws effectively could have resulted in the crumbling of Soltara.

Thankfully it didn't end that way, but such a close call with startup failure did leave me scared straight. Moving forward, I knew I had to take whatever measures were necessary to avoid such a desperate ordeal in the future. That meant, first and foremost, I had to start treating Law 12 as if my life depended on it (because it did):

Law 12: Prepare for Winter

Winter is coming.

I originally heard the warning to obey Law 12 when I attended the *Tony Robbins Business Mastery Course* in the summer of 2016. On the first day, with thousands of people waiting in the room, an enormous screen appeared that warned "WINTER IS COMING!" Quite the ominous way to kickstart a business course, but rightfully so. Tony's team went on to educate us about the history of economic seasons and how they've happened again and again.

I will save you one full day. Here is your executive summary of what I learned: it doesn't matter how long summer lasts (economic upswings). Winter always returns (economic downswings). And sometimes it's an Ice Age.

Brutal? The jungle is that way. But guess who emerges from these winters even stronger?

Answer: Lethal Entrepreneurs, who obeyed Law 12 and shifted into "sniper mode" from atop a *Winter Fortress* they built way beforehand.

As an example, think about the entrepreneurs you met in this book like Patrick Bet-David and Aubrey Marcus. Did they almost go bankrupt because of COVID? Nope. While I was clawing my way out of lockdown, they were insulated by Fortresses they'd built over the years: an armory of income streams, resources, and investments which positioned them to CRUSH IT during the economic nightmare. Or, if they desired, wait out the storm.

I confess, over the years I did not honor this Law like they did. And you saw what happened to my peace of mind and business. I paid handsomely for the error. The crazy part is, I believe COVID was only a *taste* of a full economic winter. Scary, I know, but I believe it. Just look around you. Our world is still hurting. Revolutionary forces are swelling everywhere. At the time of Costa Rica's reopening, there were wildfires in California, civil unrest around the world, Trump vs. Biden, USA vs. China. What will be next? Which conflict will overflow and trigger the next economic winter? Nobody knows, but I guarantee you something will eventually.

Obviously, you and I (and frankly anybody who relies on a healthy economy to earn a living) should want to be sitting calmly atop our protective Winter Fortress for when that day comes, but the question is how? How do we architect that lethal advantage when we're *already* super busy navigating the jungle? Energy is limited, after all.

I believe the answer to this riddle lies in Law 2: Shape Your Mind to Warfare. Recall learning that you should think like a grand-master—you should be sensing your fifteenth move—*now*, and not later. It's a simple (but extremely powerful) principle that led me to hunt the retreat with Aubrey Marcus, which played a critical role in our comeback. In that same vein, you should treat your Winter Fortress as your *One-hundredth move,* so to speak. Of course, nobody can plan that far into the future (with precision), but you don't need to. The important part is to *have* your one-hundredth move at your disposal for when the unknown arrives—like insurance, you need to be investing, bit by bit, in your future advantage while life is going relatively great.

Which brings us to a critical juncture in your startup war: **MISSION COMPLETE**.

This is a fate-defining moment for every entrepreneur, because if you cannot bring yourself to invest in your future advantage (your own Fortress) once a designated mission is won—when there's newfound excitement, momentum, or profits in the air— what makes you think you'll muster the energy to do it when the war against Failure is getting violent?

Before I end this book with how I used Soltara's "comeback momentum" as fuel for my Fortress (my one-hundredth move;

my future advantage), now is a great time to guarantee yours actually gets built too. Just as Rome wasn't built in a day, neither will your Fortress be built in a day.

Here is the secret: as you go about crushing checkpoints for your business or life, do not let your wins fizzle out and fall to waste! Make them contribute to forward motion on a separate—but parallel—route of strategic checkpoints that are preparing you for next Winter.

Did you just win your mission to hunt a star client? Great! Allocate some of those proceeds to a new brick in your Fortress. Did you finally achieve the record profits you've been dreaming of? Great job. Now add a brick. You get my point.

This means, first and foremost, that you need a vision for your unbreakable Fortress. So now you will learn about the ones that will never fail you, and happen to be rooted in the following Laws.

MULTIPLE PROFIT STREAMS

In Law 8 (Master Your Resources), you learned that COVID would end up causing Soltara to lose $1.2Mill in revenue and three years of profits. In that chapter, I needed to stop the bleeding and resuscitate our profits before it was too late. In other words, because Soltara only had *one* profit stream, this one Winter could slaughter us.

As we explored, profits are the lifeblood of your company's prosperity. No profits? No prosperity! But what is better than a business with a wildly abundant profit stream? A business with *multiple* profit streams that are, collectively, immune to a variety of economic nightmare scenarios.

The protected players of the pandemic were the ones that could switch on "pandemic-proof mode" and keep selling their offerings via the internet or delivery. Think of Uber, Amazon, or financial services. Unfortunately, Soltara did not fall in this category because we can't do ayahuasca ceremonies online.

The way you build multiple profit streams is by applying Law 8 to new "pandemic-proof" offerings within your company. Or, if you have the energy, launch an altogether new business organism that earns you profits from another marketplace. For example, as I write this chapter, I'm actively studying the landscape (refer to Law 5) of the luxury travel market because it's more immune to economic downturns and could be a reliable strategy to pandemic-proof Soltara. Whichever profit stream you end up picking, just make sure it can produce profits that are disproportionate to the level of effort needed to keep its P=R–E formula hot through Winter.

WAR CHEST OF CASH

What can your upgraded P=R–E formula get you? For one, remember in Law 7 (Plan for Snakebites) that in the middle of the pandemic, I was slapped with a $60K lawsuit from Rico, the traitor, whose snakelike tactics I had been fending off for years. Thankfully, I had been putting aside a portion of our profits just for *Snakebite Capital* (as my mentor Boyd Willat says: Hiccup Capital for business emergencies). This empowered me to lawyer-up against the snake and have him wishing he didn't betray us.

In much the same spirit, an upgraded P=R–E formula is your ticket to building a *War Chest of Cash* (a step up from having Snakebite Capital). If your Snakebite Capital helps you chop the head off business setbacks, well, your War Chest is the sniper rifle giving you an offensive edge in all Winters, emergencies, and business opportunities alike.

Unfortunately, by the time the lockdowns slammed the world, I hadn't completed my mission to build our War Chest. As a result, I desperately hunted for the emergency $620K. But imagine I completed that mission. Instead of hunting for survival, I could've used my War Chest to purchase other businesses (profit streams) for pennies on the dollar and then rebuilt them under our own brand. Or, if I desired, self-funded a hibernation for my village.

That's just one example of an offensive edge. The point is: money is power. Conversely, if you lack money—at any time—you lack power. While many complain about this fact these days, I doubt it's going to change anytime soon. In fact, I believe it'll only get more intense in the next decade. For the ones with a War Chest, the upcoming Winter could be the best thing to happen to their net worth.

INVESTMENTS

Throughout this book, I've tried my best to give you the insider's view of actual startup life, so I did not cover the COVID mayhem around the world. While Soltara's internal drama was going on, there were countless other businesses suffering—and failing—because the pandemic crippled the global economy. The US government, in particular, had to print trillions of dollars just to prop up their economy. I believe their decision was necessary to prevent the pandemic from descending into a zombie apocalypse, but that decision came with real consequences: it raised inflation (aka decreased the value of dollars)!

While the value of building a War Chest is invaluable, its power can become weakened from events like this. I'm no investment consultant, but what I understand is that to be *most* resilient during a global crisis, you want some of your War Chest parked in investments that aren't at risk of significant currency fluctuations (due to inflation) or global disruption.

So, as your War Chest is accumulating, go looking for your favorite inflation-proof investments to park some of it in. Robert Kiyosaki and Peter Schiff both love gold and silver. Mike Novogratz loves cryptocurrency. Grant Cardone loves cash flow-producing real estate. Gary Vaynerchuk loves Magic Cards. Some people hang on to art or jewelry. Your ultimate goal is to invest in something that *gains* in liquid value over the years without you having to touch it.

SOCIAL CAPITAL

Finally, there is social capital. To illustrate its game-time importance to your business, recall how in Law 10 one entrepreneur's social capital scored him *more* opportunities because of COVID. As Soltara's comeback was just beginning to rally, the world-popular entrepreneur, Patrick Bet-David received a substantial investment from me so I could be included in his mentorship program. In other words, while I was seeking answers in the world of chaos, PBD had already established himself as a man with answers.

I always knew social capital was crucial. But one lesson I learned from the pandemic was that social capital is EQUAL to money. Why? Because everybody in the world was looking for two things: cash and *attention*. If you had attention (aka followers and influential orbit), you had power.

The way you build this social capital is by tripling down on what you learned in Law 6 (especially the last two sections). Somebody like PBD has done an impressive job of this over the years by growing Valuetainment into what it is now—a podcast where he interviews the most interesting people in the world (thus, building a powerful orbit) and where he attracts attention from entrepreneurs around the world (thus, earning true fans like myself).

Whether your preferred method of building social capital is podcasting, tweeting, traditional networking, or other mediums, I recommend you put serious effort into growing that starting today. Never before in human history has social capital been so advantageous to have and—because this world is at your fingertips now—so possible to build.

That, my friend, is your final lesson of this book.

In these pages, you followed me into the unforgiving business jungle, learned the way of the Lethal Entrepreneur, met other entrepreneurs who lent me a helping hand, and watched as I made the wartime decisions that empowered Soltara to defeat Failure and keep marching to our destiny. For that, I thank you, my brothers and sisters. While our adventure together is now complete, I promise another is just beginning.

What I mean is, as part of my own winter preparation, I decided to team up with a podcast development agency in order to build the latest addition to my Winter Fortress: *The Daniel Cleland Podcast*.

Why did I choose a podcast? For one, you already learned that social capital is power.

The second reason, and the more personal one, is because of how stuck I remember feeling in my twenties. Soon after graduating from college, life started to get—how shall I say boring and repetitive?—and I began agonizing over "Is this all I'm going to do for the next fifty years until I retire and go in the dirt?"

The thought made me shudder. It was a lifestyle I didn't want to submit to. Flash forward to now, after journeying out of that matrix. I feel I've collected hard lessons about what's required to transition away from that cookie-cutter lifestyle, as well as lessons about entrepreneurial thinking, plant medicines, international traveling, and ex-pat living. And you know what? I don't want to keep them in my head. I want to share them with dreamers like you, so you'll become not just a Lethal Entrepreneur, but a lethal individual. That podcast adventure is happening at DanielCleland.com.

When I teamed up with the agency to get it locked in (back when I was kickstarting Soltara's comeback), I decided to ask

Patrick Bet-David what he recommended I should do to make it extraordinarily valuable to my audience. With over two million followers on his podcast, I thought who better to ask?

Of all things, PBD boiled the secret down to one thing: *Don't be boring.*

That was all I needed to hear. Along my journey, I've been blessed to become friends with very non-boring, legendary humans of the world. Many of whom created impressive lives for themselves. Many of whom you have met in this story. Many of whom agreed to come on my podcast and share their wisdom with trailblazers like you.

I am thrilled we can begin another chapter together by listening to their amazing perspectives on how to live the good life. To name a few, you'll be learning directly from people like Aubrey Marcus, Brian Rose, Dennis McKenna, Dorian Yates, and even the man himself, Patrick Bet-David.

Of course, I cannot forget the person this book opened with: the guitarist I've been looking up to since I was sixteen, Logan Mader. This book began with us meeting up at his reunion tour, sipping rum together backstage, and agreeing to reunite at Soltara's March ceremony.

As you know, COVID had different plans. I was forced to cancel all Soltara's retreats and undergo this Hero's Journey. Back then, in March of 2020, I believed nothing good would come from that soul-crushing disappointment. I couldn't have guessed it was going to make for an even better story after all. Logan agreed to come on my podcast. It was a podcast I wouldn't have brought to the world if not for the wild turn of events.

Now it's your turn. The power is in your hands. Whatever your circumstances are right now, you can bet they won't get better unless you take massive and relentless action. The opportunities at your fingertips right now, if left alone, will expire. Seasons change. Winter is en route, and you need to make hay while the sun shines. So, map your route, rally the village, and grab your spear. The time to kill is motherfucking NOW!

EPILOGUE

How to Unleash a Year of Excellence

February 2022–460 days after lockdowns ended

Ability is God-given, prowess is earned.

—John Harbaugh

IN THE ONE YEAR AFTER COMPLETING THE MANUSCRIPT FOR THIS book, there have been exciting changes at Soltara: frustrating snakebites, hunts, and deals made, others lost, and wave after wave of social, economic, and political influences storming in from the zeitgeist. In other words, the jungle hasn't stopped for anybody. It never will. As this book nears publication, I want to explore a final question that should help you face it forever like a savage: how do you apply these 12 Laws to unleash a full year of excellence, not merely short-lived success?

This book taught you each Law one by one—a crucial milestone. But it isn't enough to know them individually. Like all great performers, you have to unleash all or parts of your know-how

179

on command, again and again, without too much thinking. The key is gradually turning these Laws into your second nature, your modus operandi, and your way of existence. Using one case study of how my life changed after writing this book, following are four rules for fostering that.

HARDWIRE EACH LAW

Nine months after the lockdowns ended, Logan Mader (the guitar hero and producer I introduced in the beginning of this book) finally flew to meet me in Costa Rica, but not for an ayahuasca ceremony (as was our original plan before the lockdowns). Rocking his look of a true guitar legend, Logan arrived here to help my band to produce our debut album and prepare *us* to go on tour! In a moment I'll catch you up on the state of Soltara, but I think this creative project is the perfect example to explore, because it wasn't even on my radar when I began writing this book in 2020. It goes to show that you need a built-in operating system for attacking *any* project. When engaged with a new or existing mission, any given week could feel akin to close-range combat, with each Law coming into play in quick succession.

This brings me to the first rule: hardwire each Law into your psyche. All great performers do this. Think of Mayweather, Joe Rogan, or even Logan Mader himself. While performing in front of thousands and as pressure heats up, they aren't thinking HOW to apply their techniques. The HOWs are ingrained. They are ready to unleash. This is why I felt OK asking Logan to produce our album. I didn't have a full band yet, nor much experience playing live before, but I knew the Laws were hard-wired and could bear the weight of the project. That's your goal too.

The good news is you already know how to do this. Once upon a time you felt awkward learning to walk, but you were hardwired to walk. You repeated that hardwiring process with hundreds of other skills. You used your own style, of course. Take the same approach here.

Which Law do you need to go from crawling, to walking, to running? For example, maybe you're blazing bright with a Fuck Yes! Vision and mission (Law 4 and Law 5), but fizzling out on execution (Law 9 and Law 10) or wartime decisions (Law 2) or influencing (Law 3). Reread the respective Law. Make it your own. Get confident using it on the fly.

Jesse Radford (drummer, head chef at Soltara, and my best friend since kindergarten) and I began reinvigorating our old band in November of 2020, just as a fun hobby. By April of 2021, we were back to jamming like the old days, and we were really starting to have fun. That's when I got the crazy idea to invite Logan to Costa Rica to record a demo of the songs we were writing for our budding new band we coined Savage Existence.

Once Logan gave the yes, each Law started jumping onto the scene for what we began calling "Operation Become Rock Star." My personal vision was clear right from the start. I wanted to play for 30,000 people in a stadium. Bold and extremely unlikely to happen, but that's the Fuck Yes! Vision that was getting me fired up. Either way, I knew I wanted to write music and then go play it live for audiences around the world. Instantly Jesse and I dedicated ourselves to a ninety-day window to practice our butts off (*Law 9 to the extreme*). By the time Logan actually arrived, our music actually took him by surprise! He didn't expect us to sound so good! From there we got to work. Logan was working his magic behind the studio glass, Jesse was on the drums, and I was on guitar. We recorded the album's instrumentals in just six days (*Law 10 to the extreme*).

SHIFT GEARS

The second rule is to shift between the Laws with prowess like a savage. It's the dynamism between the Laws—not one magic push—that accelerates your projects and business. In any one week, you might need to crank one, two, or three more of the Laws, and then later downshift to others. Played together in this fashion, you will build and keep enormous momentum.

After recording instrumentals, we did just that. We needed to start fleshing out Vision and Strategy for Operation Become Rock Star (*shifting to Law 4 and Law 5*). Knowing that Logan was a deep-sea fishing enthusiast, I planned a fishing adventure in Quepos where we stayed at the same hotel that I drove to during the events of Law 7 when I healed my snakebites, and had my phone call with Dorian Yates. It was surreal to be there with Logan and Jesse now under a totally different set of circumstances. The morning of, we were on the high seas catching *massive* red snappers and handfuls of rabbit fish. Once we returned to the hotel, the staff kindly prepared them in a feast fit for kings! While chowing down on our seafood smorgasbord, Logan focused on the importance of recruiting a vocalist, bassist, and second guitar player (upshifting to Law 6 ASAP) before getting too excited about touring. He put a special emphasis on the vocalist; our album couldn't be finished without it.

Jesse seemed discouraged. I understood why. Apparently, it was going to take a long time to find the rest of our bandmates. Logic seemed to suggest that we shouldn't spend so much cash and energy on a dream so hard to achieve. But I, on the other hand, felt ready to destroy the world with our music. I think this is a salient point. Whenever you're investing your energies into a set of Laws, I've noticed that inertia can trap you there and make you feel stuck in neutral as you start backsliding. For example, we knew there was a lot more into shifting the Laws before we discovered band members and crushed the touring process. It was a daunting process in some ways. But the trick, I believe, is to distrust the inertia and trust whichever Law(s) is called for at that moment.

"The time to kill is now, boys." I heard myself say this to Logan and Jesse. While we'd been fleshing all this out over the grand fish dinner, my mind was remembering a couple days earlier when our studio gave me the phone number of a professionally trained vocalist named Anton Darusso who lives here in Costa Rica. I suspected maybe he was the right fit for Savage Existence. It was a long shot, but I also knew Law 10 had produced so many positive outcomes in my life. The magic ingredient had always been to act with urgency, not talk myself out of it, not find excuses, and not get sidetracked. So I trusted Law 10 and messaged Anton immediately from the dinner table.

Later that evening, Anton and I were on a video call exploring alignment. During that thirty-minute conversation, I knew I needed to shift into a bit of Law 6 (checking if he's masterful), a bit of Law 3 (advancing both our destinies), and a bit of Law 4 and Law 5, (conveying our mission with Operation Become Rock Star).

Many details went into our conversation, but the overriding emotion was that of a strong chemistry on just about every point. He informed me that he'd just finished rehearsals for the Philharmonic Orchestra in San Jose, where he was gearing up to perform three concerts for Metallica cover songs in front of one thousand people. Turns out he'd been a professional singer for twenty years and toured the world with some of the greats like Ronnie James Dio! He seemed like a great fit because of his formal training and touring experience that Jesse and I lacked as self-taught musicians. By the end of our call, we found the right balance of Law 3, and Anton agreed to be our vocalist. The cherry on top? Anton assured me he knew many contacts in the music industry and could easily find us a second guitarist and bass player for live performances.

MAINTAIN A POSITIVE MENTAL ATTITUDE

One week later, we were all in the studio again and tracking vocals. Logan was sure we needed at least five days. But Anton was so professional and efficient that we tracked vocals for all eleven songs in two days! "This was the Guinness book of world records for vocal recording. I've never seen anything like it," Logan said, looking genuinely impressed.

We were beyond pleased with how Anton's voice meshed with our instrumentals. Our band always had a spectrum of sounds ranging from clean melodic riffs, to slow groove metal, to fast, thrash metal. Anton hit the melodies, and he also hit the ranges of metal rock as far-reaching as the low-pitch growling, common-in-death metal. The album came together in a way that takes listeners on an engaging journey of primal emotion–rightfully titled *ANIMALS*.

You can imagine how ecstatic we felt to be part of such momentum. We were manifesting our childhood dreams and about to turn our minds to touring. Of course, that's when Law 7 attacked from the bushes: $10K worth of our band equipment was stolen the next week by the security guards I trusted. Infuriating as that was, I had to accept fault for divulging my door code to one of them, knowing full well I'd seen things go missing in the past. I wasn't watching like a hawk, and I got bitten. Suffice it to say, they were fired, and we applied technology to eliminate the need for door guards at all. The silver lining was that I had to buy a new guitar, and I got a doozy.

This brings me to the next rule: Maintain a Positive Mental Attitude. No matter how difficult or improbable things seem, you have to believe you can achieve things before you actually do. You CANNOT talk yourself out of it. You CANNOT fixate on all the reasons why it might not work. You CANNOT allow bumps in the road to destroy your spirit. Expel that shit from your mind! As soon as you notice doubtful thoughts creeping into your consciousness, banish them forever.

I repeat, DO NOT LET DOUBT INFECT YOUR MIND this year. Even if there are justifiable reasons for it–like our $10K snakebite, or the seemingly daunting process of completing our album. Convince yourself that you can achieve whatever you want anyway.

When I think about it, our music is really dedicated to maintaining that exact attitude. As you go about your year, remember that we made it for people like you. More than a name, Savage Existence is a *lifestyle*. It's fuel for unleashing your raw human potential. I understand that not everyone loves heavy metal, but I believe our music transcends genre, race, and creed because of the universal human spirit within it. Its message is to be strong, overcome your challenges, and have zero shame being the Predator (owning your day), not Prey (infected by victim mentality).

OWN THE YEAR

The final note I want to leave with you is less of a rule and more of a belief. Every entrepreneur I know is hellbent on making the absolute best of their year. We have a deep and persistent fear of squandering our opportunities. So we seize it with everything we've got. Nobody knows for sure what happens after this life, but we do know we all get one shot. And that shot has an ever-shrinking window before it's gone forever. Day by day, week by week, year by year, it shrinks until it's sealed shut. As you put these Laws to use—shifting between them and maintaining the Positive Mental Attitude of a predator—think of the next year as a gift to be seized upon and experienced to the utmost. Make it your best year yet.

That was the silent but lethal belief system driving us to make *ANIMALS* in just three weeks, and also behind me leading Soltara as best I could. By now you're probably wondering what happened to Soltara after the lockdowns. In much the same style of unleashing the Laws for our debut album, I was unleashing the Laws for Soltara the whole time. One Law led to another, and now Soltara is in quite the advantageous position compared to when the pandemic threatened to subvert everything we had built.

As I write this closing chapter, we are sitting on explosive growth with hundreds of people on the waitlist. After reopening with Aubrey Marcus's *Road to Realization Retreat* in December 2020, demand kept rising and left us sold out of retreats through 2021. Delta actually evolved to become a *$5Mill* project on a different property ninety minutes from Soltara, in another stunning beachfront location on the open Pacific. The $620K I needed to raise became $5Mill—a good chunk of what we're funding internally from our explosive post-lockdown success. On top of that, we eventually refunded all those people who wanted their money back. Wages for the village are at their highest they've ever been, and our Masterful Tribe has never been stronger and more driven.

As for Aubrey's retreat? Although he initially did the retreat to help us smash through COVID, the experience blew him away. He referred to Soltara as "impeccable" and asked me to help orchestrate private retreats every six to nine months with his closest tribe members and favorite Shaman from Peru. In fact, as I prepare this epilogue, we are just a few months from Aubrey's third *rendezvous* with us!

On their first retreat, Jesse and I played three songs from our album for the intrepid few who dared come down to the infamous guard shack to check us out: 1) A Thousand Pounds of Trainwreck; 2) Animals; 3) Demons. All groovy, upbeat metal songs that are easy to catch on to. It was amazing seeing their responses to our music that, just three weeks earlier, wasn't even ready! They were jumping around, moshing, and unleashing their inner savage. Mehcad Brooks (the actor who played Jax in the latest *Mortal Kombat* movie) was part of that close-knit group and told us afterward, "That was exactly what we needed."

On that note, I hope this book was what you needed. It was never the plan for it to come full circle like this, but I suppose that's a testament to these Laws. As I look into my horizon, I see my company Soltara en route to its Peacetime era. My band Savage Existence is en route to our *second* tour in Mexico. This time it's with one of my all-time favorite bands, Sepultura, and we've already recorded our second album *Matricide*, which will launch later this year, so keep an eye out. I still find it mind-blowing to think about how far I've come and what's actually possible when the *12 Laws of the Jungle* are applied with full force: **ANYTHING!**

Where are you en route to? Let me know at dan@danielcleland. com. I look forward to staying in touch. Until then, I bid you adieu and wish you all the power in the world.

Godspeed!

APPENDIX

Jungle Prep Questionnaire

WHAT IS YOUR STARTUP ENDGAME?

SOME FOUNDERS WANT TO VENTURE INTO THE STARTUP JUNGLE and eventually sell the company at a profit (they don't want to stay in the game forever). Others dream of stabilizing a company and managing it full time (they are more interested in the lifestyle than in constant growth and challenge). For them the jungle never ends, but it gets easier once they have strong assets, no debt, a great team, and an established brand. Then you have founders like myself (in love with the art of leading a startup through early-stage wartime battles, but then passing the mantle to another worthy leader once the time is right).

Which do you really want? Be honest. Visualize it. Bring it into your mind's eye. Feel it. I will expand on this in Law 4 (Set Your Destination), but for now, make sure you are headed in the right general direction.

WHAT IS YOUR JUNGLE'S DENSITY (RISK PROFILE)?

Some jungles are sparse with risk. Others are dense with it. Your job is to understand the risk profile of your market. Understand key factors like market value; top one to three competitors; regulatory hurdles; funding limitations; changing economic conditions; logistic complexity; labor availability. Remember, you are more prone to getting lost in dense jungles, so really study it. For example, doing business in South America is no walk in the park. It is a dense jungle. The silver lining? Once you crack the code and learn how to navigate a dense jungle, the upside can be very prosperous.

WHAT CHECKPOINTS WILL YOU HIT?

The last place you want to be is lost in a jungle. You must know the routes, topography, biohazards, sinkholes, quicksand, and every other potential landmark you want to successfully cross.

It's no different with your startup. When will you slam dunk your first dream client? And your second? When will you reach your fiscal breakeven point? When will you get that Holy Grail PR article or podcast appearance? When will you reach profitability? When will you be able to pay dividends (if you choose to)? When will you be able to give back to your community (if you choose to)? What checkpoints haven't you accounted for yet?

WHAT GEAR DO YOU NEED?

Your gear keeps you alive. The essentials are your compass, map, expedition party, and machete. But will you bring a tent to sleep in that will protect you from the water? What about mosquito nets?

Obviously, a mosquito net isn't going to do your business much good (unless you're in the mosquito net business). But what tech or resources are foundational to your business? Mac or PC? Samsung or iPhone? Salesforce or Intuit? What vehicles? Lease or buy? Office space? Lease or buy? How many square feet? Run a pros and cons analysis of which services you want to keep in-house, and which ones to outsource. Make a plan and budget.

WHERE ARE THE DANGERS?

In a real jungle, you should know the lurking dangers. Brown scorpions? Vipers? Boa constrictors? Are they venomous?

Similarly, in the startup jungle, you must anticipate dangers. Are there competitors who will play dirty? Do you have personal issues that might come up unexpectedly and limit your engagement? Is there a tumultuous political environment or corrupt operatives that might inhibit your progress like in my extortion crisis? Is your industry ripe for technological disruption or exposed to changes in global stability?

Fuck Yes!
Life Questionnaire

- **How old are you?** (Is your vision happening when you're still young, or is it like mine when I envisioned my old age?)

- **How do you look?** (Do you see the "you" of right now, or do you see a different "you" of the future?)

- **Where are you standing?** (Mentally place yourself in the space where you'll be when your vision becomes reality.)

- **What is the weather like?** (How does the air feel? What is the temperature on your skin? Is the sun shining? Is it a light drizzle, or is it fresh autumn air in your nostrils?)

- **What is surrounding you?** (Imagine your surroundings in exquisite detail. Don't be shy!)

- **What is your main emotion?** (How do you feel in that future moment? Accomplished? Proud? In love? Overjoyed? At peace?)

- **Why that feeling?** (What's the reason WHY you're feeling this way in your future moment?)

- **Who is with you?** (Are you surrounded by friends or one of your heroes? The spouse of your dreams? Maybe two or three spouses of your dreams?)

- **How do they feel?** (What do they feel when they look at you? What kind of relationship do you have with them in your future? Do they admire you? Love you? Trust you?)

- **What are you doing together?** (What are you doing together in your future? Chilling? Dancing? Boating? Playing music in front of a packed stadium? Making love?)

- **What do you have?** (i.e., a home? Tesla? BMW? Nothing except your backpack and a motorcycle? A family and a golden retriever?)

- **How much is in your bank?** (i.e., $100K? $1Mill? $1B?)

- **What is your legacy?** (How does the world know you? What will they remember you for?)

- **How does it feel to look back at your legacy?** (Did you earn it? Do you love it? Are you happy with what you've done in life?)

The Way-Forward Questionnaire

- **What is your mission?** Get clear on your mission and make sure you are directing your observations toward that.

- **What is the bad news?** What are the threats facing you or your organization, in order of lethality? Get real. Don't bullshit yourself. You need to see the battlefield in 20/20 vision.

- **What's the good news?** What are your strengths? What "aces in the hole" do you have? Who are your powerful allies? How is your team? What's your cash flow situation like? How is your credit? What season is it in the market?

- **What must happen to reach your destination?** What are the critical one to five moves that must be made so you can accomplish your mission?

- **What is your Plan A?** Mastermind a Plan A that takes into account the bad news and the good news and what your mission can accomplish.

- **Assumptions?** Think about the factors you assume are given but could hurt if they got taken away.

- **Risks?** What ugly serpents are waiting for you in the bushes? Who's out to get you? What could go wrong? What do you need to keep an eye on? What could take you out completely?

- **Next Steps?** Write out your action steps and get to work.

Strategic Checkpoints Table

LOOK AT THE NEXT YEAR OF YOUR LIFE AND BREAK YOUR Plan A (from your Way Forward) into four quarters: Q1 to Q4. Identify three significant and Strategic Checkpoints for each of those four quarters of the next year. Add those checkpoints into a spreadsheet you can see every single day.

Quarter 1	Quarter 2	Quarter 3	Quarter 4
Checkpoint 1	Checkpoint 1	Checkpoint 1	Checkpoint 1
Checkpoint 2	Checkpoint 2	Checkpoint 2	Checkpoint 2
Checkpoint 3	Checkpoint 3	Checkpoint 3	Checkpoint 3

Attack those checkpoints with extreme prejudice and make sure you're moving toward them every single day. Let them guide your movements. Never let them out of your sight.

Traits of a Masterful Nuclear Tribe

ARE THEY MASTERFUL?

LIKE A NEW BANDMATE, YOUR CANDIDATE SHOULD HAVE mastery over his or her individual domain. They will become a vital prong of your company machine, so their unique and complementary talent must plug perfectly into that machine, making it stronger, faster, and more appealing to customers.

ARE THEY LOYAL?

Loyalty keeps the tribe solid. Hate him or love him, former US President Donald Trump was famous for demanding loyalty from everybody in his orbit. I'm sure this is after having been betrayed in the past and learning how fatal it can be for business. You must feel you can trust tribe members to show up, play strong, and not leave you high and dry just because the going gets tough.

ARE THEY DIVERSE?

I am not suggesting that you hire unqualified people to create diversity for diversity's sake. I am talking about cultivating diversity of life experience and perspective among your tribe. Have you ever felt stuck on a problem until somebody blows your mind with a unique point of view? That is the power of true diversity. A candidate who diversifies the collective consciousness of your tribe will give your startup machine a competitive advantage in the formulation of strategies and decisions.

Acknowledgments

PEOPLE MAY LOOK AT A GUY LIKE ME (OR ANY NUMBER OF GUYS like me) and think that we're overachievers. In reality, that's not true. The reality is that we're surrounded by generous and talented people who share their skills and time to bring common goals to fruition.

I could never write this book by myself while running Soltara. The first person I need to thank is Matt Cartagena, the coauthor of this book. It's because of him that these entrepreneurial principles of my operating system were distilled, defined, and immortalized into this book. Thank you, Matt.

Second, I wouldn't have had the time to work on this book unless I had such a stellar team running Soltara. Specifically, Melissa Stangl, Ezio Cabalceta, Todd Roberts. and my father, Charlie Cleland. They are the ones who aren't able to check out every couple of months and take time off. They're the ones who are in it to win it.

Third, I have to acknowledge the thousands of people from around the world who've made their choice to better themselves and take on the full responsibility of their lives, and fortunately that included participation in our programs at Soltara and, previous to that, at Pulse. Without you, I would have nothing to write about at all.

Last, I'd like to thank the legendary mentors and influential leaders whose examples I've utilized in this book, and some of whom have added kind words of their own: Patrick Bet-David. Aubrey Marcus. Dennis McKenna. Brian Rose. I appreciate you.

Printed in Great Britain
by Amazon

12721975R00123